ON

GÖDEL

Jaakko Hintikka
Boston University

Australia • Canada • Mexico • Singapore • Spain
United Kingdom • United States

Printed in the United States of America
2 3 4 5 6 7 03 02 01

For permission to use material from this text, contact us:
Web: http://www.thomsonrights.com
Fax: 1-800-730-2215
Phone: 1-800-730-2214

For more information, contact:
Wadsworth/Thomson Learning, Inc.
10 Davis Drive
Belmont, CA 94002-3098
USA
http://www.wadsworth.com

ISBN: 0-534-57595-1

Table of Contents

PREFACE

Kurt Gödel (1906-1978) was one of the most important logicians ever. His results, especially his proof to the effect that every axiom system of elementary arithmetic is deductively incomplete, have changed - or ought to have changed - our way of thinking about the foundations of mathematics forever. Gödel also had interesting philosophical ideas and ideals, prominently including the ideal of rationality. Yet his own life reminds one of the title of a book on game theory, *The Paradoxes of Rationality*. Gödel believed in the ideal of rationality also outside logic and philosophy, but he conducted his own personal life in a manner that easily strikes one as absurdly irrational. He discovered the most radically new results in logic in the twentieth century, but preferred to conduct his own research within some conventionally accepted framework. The paradoxes extend to Gödel's influence. His best known results, especially his first incompleteness theorem just mentioned, have often been interpreted in a way diametrically opposite to his own convictions.

It is thus easy to convince oneself that Gödel's work needs to be put in a new, sharper light even in a logico-mathematical perspective, let alone in a philosophical and historical perspective. This volume is an attempt to take a first step towards such a re-evaluation. I will suggest that recent developments in logic and foundations of mathematics help to put Gödel's work in a partly new perspective.

In writing this book, I have made ample use of earlier literature prominently including John W. Dawson's biography, the writings of the late Hao Wong, and the perceptive work of Solomon Feferman.

However, I am alone responsible for the interpretations offered in the following pages.

1

PROLOGUE: THE KÖNIGSBERG BOMBSHELL

The subject of this book, Kurt Gödel (1906 – 1978) was not only a great logician with interesting philosophical ideas. It is a measure of Gödel's status that the most important moment of his career is the most important moment in the history of twentieth-century logic, maybe in the history of logic in general. That moment opens a window to Gödel's achievements, their reception and their significance. It is therefore in order to have a look at what happened.

This *Sternstunde* was October 7, 1930. The setting was a conference on the foundations of mathematics in Königsberg on October 5-7, 1930. This meeting was not a sectarian one. On the first day, a worthy spokesman of each of the three main current approaches to the philosophical and conceptual basis of mathematics gave a presentation of the position of his school. Rudolf Carnap presented "The main ideas of logicism", A. Heyting "The intuitionistic foundation of mathematics" and the great John von Neumann, representing David Hilbert's school in Göttingen, spoke of "The axiomatic foundation of mathematics." As a chronicler notes, a fourth address by Friedrich Waismann representing Wittgenstein's position was added to these in the last minute, but in the end it was agreed that Wittgenstein's ideas were not presented in a form ripe for debate. (See Dawson 1997, pp. 68-71.)

On the second day, three other established philosophers and mathematicians presented major papers, followed by three twenty-minute contributed ones. One of the latter was by a young logician from Vienna named Kurt Gödel. It was an elegant albeit compressed paper, but unsurprising – or so everybody seems to have thought. What Gödel did was to show what many foundationalists had already assumed, namely, that our basic working logic – or, rather, what has nearly universally been taken to be such a logic – is complete in one natural sense of completeness. This basic logic was then known as predicate calculus or the lower functional calculus but is in our days usually referred to as (ordinary) first-order logic, sometimes also as quantification theory. Its nature and the nature of Gödel's completeness proof for it will be explained in greater detail in Chapter 3. Suffice it to say here that its primitive logical constants can be taken to be the two quantifiers "there exists an individual x such that" in short ($\exists$x), and "for each individual y", in short ($\forall$y), negation $\sim$, conjunction &, and disjunction $\lor$. The x's and y's of the quantifiers is understood to "range over" all the members of some given domain of individuals or "universe of discourse." What Gödel showed in full detail is that whenever a formula of such a first-order logic cannot be disproved, in the sense that its negation cannot be proved, it can be interpreted so as to be true. It follows that, whenever a formula is true on every possible interpretation ("in every model"), it can be proved. This universal provability is what is here meant by completeness: all logical truths are provable. And the notion of provability used here is a purely mechanical one, the derivability of the formula in question from explicitly formulated "axioms of logic" by means by purely mechanical "rules of logical inference." These rules can in principle be programmed into a computer. Gödel's completeness proof thus encouraged logicians in that it seemed to show that the proof methods that they had developed are as good as they could possibly be, at least where it comes to being able to prove somehow everything that has to be proved.

To return to Königsberg, the third day was devoted to a general discussion of the foundations of mathematics in the light of the talks heard in the preceding two days and of other relevant results. In that discussion, our young Viennese logician made a startling statement. As will be explained, the Königsberg meeting took place in the shadow of

Hilbert's program of safeguarding mathematical axiom systems by proving their formal consistency. Gödel pointed out that such a consistency is not enough. Even is no materially false statements are provable in an axiom system, it can happen that not all materially true theorems are provable. And not only can this happen. The young man from Vienna announced the result that such an incompleteness not only prevails but is unavoidable. As Gödel formulated his point:

> One can (assuming the [formal] consistency of classical mathematics) even give examples of propositions (and indeed, of such of the type of Goldbach and Fermat) which are really contextually [materially] true but unprovable in the formal system of classical mathematics.

Gödel had indeed proved such a result. This result is known as his first incompleteness theorem. It is arguably one of the most important and challenging discoveries in twentieth-century science, comparable with Einstein's theory of relativity or Heisenberg's uncertainty relation. Some writers have called it an "earthquake" in the foundations of logic and mathematics. It put in one fell swoop into a new light the entire learned discussion of the preceding two and a half days – or perhaps a more appropriate metaphor would be a new darkness from which the entire philosophy of mathematics is only now, seventy years later, slowly beginning to emerge.

Even before we have had a closer look at the two results that Gödel presented or announced in Königsberg we can appreciate the revolutionary character of his incompleteness theorem. What this theorem showed that the entire earlier methodology of mathematics was unsatisfactory. Ever since the days of ancient Greek mathematicians like Euclid, the study of any one branch of mathematics was thought of as taking ideally the form of an axiomatic theory. The idea is that the basic truths of that branch are summed up in a number of axioms. If that axiom system is complete, all the other truths of that part of mathematics can be derived purely logically. Examples of such axiom systems (whether complete or not, is not the question here) include Euclid's *Elements* and from more recent times David Hilbert's *Foundations of Geometry* (1899). What Gödel showed that this strategy does not work even in the case of as simple and basic mathematical theory as elementary arithmetic, that is, the study of the structure of the natural numbers 0, 1, 2, ... in terms of addition, multiplication and the successor relation. No matter what axiom system

3

you write down, and no matter what purely formal rules of logical inference you choose, there will be true statements about natural numbers which are not derivable from those axioms by these rules. Theorem-proving is often thought of as the be-all and end-all of the mathematical method. But from Gödel's results it seems to follow that it cannot be all that there is to mathematics.

What was the reaction of the learned audience to Gödel's momentous announcement? Was there a chorus of objections and questions? Did the good mathematics professors rush to telephones to convey this sensational news to their colleagues and students? The unsurprising truth is: nothing like this happened. Gödel's result was so new and so puzzling methodologically that it did not sink in immediately. The speaker who tried to sum up the discussion did not even mention Gödel's result. This incomprehension was not even alleviated by the fact that Gödel had discussed his result with Carnap in Vienna prior to the Königsberg meeting.

The only exception to this lack of reaction was John von Neumann. He lived up to his legendary reputation of immediately grasping any mathematical idea. (It is told that he could walk in halfway through a research talk in mathematics and five minutes later begin to correct the speaker.) John von Neumann grasped immediately Gödel's line of thought and buttonholed Gödel after the discussion. He went home and began to expound Gödel's result to others. Furthermore, he soon noticed a truly remarkable corollary to Gödel's result. What Gödel had done was to give a conditional proof: If an axiomatic system containing elementary arithmetic is consistent, then one can find a specific proposition G that is true but unprovable in that system. What von Neumann realized is that Gödel's proof itself can be carried out in a system of elementary arithmetic. Hence, if that system could be proved to be consistent in the elementary arithmetic, one could after all prove in the system that G is true. But by Gödel's very own first incompleteness theorem, G is unprovable in that system. Hence the initial assumption must be wrong, in other words, the consistency of the system cannot be proved in the system itself. In particular, the consistency of as weak a system as elementary arithmetic cannot be proved in elementary arithmetic.

John von Neumann conveyed this result to Gödel, who politely informed von Neumann that he had reached the same result earlier. This result is known as Gödel's second incompleteness theorem. It was the first one of Gödel's results that was received special attention. It was perceived to upset the great project in the foundations of mathematics by David Hilbert, arguably the greatest mathematician of that time. In order to understand the impact of Gödel's results, it is therefore in order to survey the situation in the philosophy of mathematics in 1931–and later. This will be done in Chapter 4.

Likewise, as a part of the background of a discussion of Gödel's results, we also need to know more about his life and personality.

II

GÖDEL'S LIFE AND PERSONALITY

Gödel's discoveries were major events in the history of logic and mathematics. It was seen how dramatic his incompleteness theorems originally were. In contrast, Gödel's life story is not very rich in dramatic events. Even the most extraordinary feature of the Gödel saga, the cause of his death, was a non-event rather than any striking act of God or nature or man. According to his death certificate, he died of "malnutrition and inanition" brought about by "personality disturbance." In plain English, he starved himself to death.

We are obviously dealing with a most unusual person. However, the external circumstances of his life do not contribute very much to understanding Gödel's personality. Kurt Friedrich Gödel was born on April 28, 1906 in Brno in Moravia, in what now is the Czech Republic. His parents were of German rather than Czech origin, however. His father, who was a director and part owner of a textile factory, died in 1929 before Kurt Gödel's career got started. Kurt's mother was a well-educated, competent housewife. He had an older brother, Rudolf Gödel, who became a successful physician.

Kurt Gödel was always close to his mother. Probably the only major thing he did against her wishes was to marry Adele Porkert on September 20, 1938. According to Gödel's biographer, in his parents' eyes "Adele had many faults: Not only was she a divorcée, older than their son by more than six years but she was Catholic, she came from a lower-class family, her face was distinguished by a port wine stain, and, worst of all she was a *dancer,* employed according to several accounts at a Viennese night club" (Dawson 1994, p. 34). The marriage

6

was nevertheless a happy one. Adele shielded Kurt from the outside world and took care of him, and not only as a homemaker. When on one occasion the two were assaulted in Vienna by a couple of Nazi rowdies, it was Adele who beat the attackers to retreat with her umbrella.

After a solid school education in Brno, Gödel entered the University of Vienna in 1924. He described to Hao Wang (in the third person) his student years as follows:

> ...[H]e went, in 1924, to Vienna to study [theoretical] physics at the University. His interest in precision led him from physics to mathematics and to mathematical logic. He enjoyed much the lectures by P. Furtwängler [cousin of the famous conductor] on number theory and developed an interest in this subject which was, for example, relevant to his application of the Chinese remainder theorem in expressing primitive recursive functions in terms of addition and multiplication. In 1926 he transferred to mathematics and coincidentally became a member of the M. Schlick Circle. However, he has never been a positivist, but only accepted some of their theses even at that time. Later on, he moved further and further away from them. He completed his formal studies at the University before the summer of 1929. He also attended during this period philosophical lectures by Heinrich Gomperz whose father was famous in Greek philosophy.

Gödel's dissertation adviser was Hans Hahn, an excellent mathematician with strong philosophical interests and one of the central figures of the famous group of philosophers, mathematicians, and scientists known as the Vienna Circle. This positivistic group in what is referred to in the Hao Wang quotation.

After Gödel's pathbreaking results announced in Königsberg, he became a Dozent (lecturer) at the University of Vienna in 1933. He visited the United States in 1933-34, 1935, and 1938-39. Even though he was not Jewish, the situation in Vienna became more and more unpleasant, especially after the annexation of Austria by the Nazi Germany in 1938. As a consequence, Kurt and Adele left Vienna for the United States on January 18, 1940 arriving in San Francisco on March 4. Gödel worked at the Institute of Advanced Study (IAS) in

Princeton, became a permanent member in 1946 and professor in 1953. At the IAS, Gödel became a friend of a famous fellow member, Albert Einstein.

Gödel's mental health was a fragile one. He suffered repeatedly from depression, paranoia, and hypochondria, and was hospitalized more than once. He distrusted doctors, and often refused to be treated for his bodily problems. When Adele was hospitalized in 1977, Kurt's paranoia got the upper hand. He refused medical treatment and even his friends' help. His suspicions of much of his ordinary diet developed into serious anorexia to which he succumbed on January 14, 1978.

Gödel's mental problems are not as such relevant to understanding his work in logic and mathematics or his philosophical ideas. However, in spite of the highly abstract character of Gödel's accomplishments, I believe that understanding his character helps us to understand his attitude toward his own ideas and even his philosophical ideas. Gödel's paranoia was a reflection of his general insecurity. This insecurity was of a rather specific character. What Gödel needed was a safe accepted framework within which to operate. Within that framework, Gödel could give free reign to his marvelous critical and constructive intelligence. However, he never challenged that framework seriously be it intellectually or politically. In a perceptive essay, Solomon Feferman has spoken of Gödel's "conviction and caution." Feferman notes the consequences of Gödel's "caution":

> It seemed to me that he [Gödel] could well have been more centrally involved in the development of the fundamental concepts of modern logic—truth and compatibility—than he was.

> ...throughout the 1930's, he shied away from the new concept as an object of study as opposed to new concepts as a tool for obtaining the results.[my italics]

To make the new concepts "objects of study" would have meant to transcend the old framework within which logicians had been working whereas using these as tools for obtaining new results can happen within the received framework.

Gödel's attitude is vividly illustrated by the story of his

application for a United States citizenship in 1947. As any other applicant, he was expected to answer questions about the American system of government, including the United States constitution. Here was an accepted framework of the kind within which Gödel liked to operate. He put his ingenuity to work, and in no time found an incompleteness proof of sorts, in that he devised an involved way in which the United States could be turned into a dictatorship completely constitutionally. Of course, nothing was further from his mind than an actual subversion of the United States constitution. But his friends at IAS realized that the examining judge might not realize this, and tried to distract him. However, at the crucial moment Gödel could not keep his mind and his mouth off the subject. Fortunately, his friends present managed to join forces with the enlightened judge to maintain a semblance of normality in the proceedings. To add poignancy to the tragicomedy, one of the two friends was Albert Einstein.

This story has a sequel of sorts, illustrating Gödel's need of a strong safe social order. In 1952, Einstein reported to a colleague with a straight face, "You know, Gödel has really gone completely crazy." What more could he have done? "He voted for General Eisenhower!"

As can be expected on the basis of these glimpses, Gödel's views were – both in logic and outside of it – a mixture of extraordinary sharp insights and strange, sometimes paranoid beliefs. In logic and the foundations of mathematics, his instant insight was so sharp and quick that a visitor often had the impression that you could not tell him anything that was news to him. Yet at the same time, he sincerely believed in a version of the old ontological argument for God's existence. In philosophy, he spontaneously recognized Leibniz's genius. At the same time, he believed that certain powers-to-be had tried to suppress not only Leibniz's ideas but also his writings.

Even in this strange assortment of views, Gödel's genius is usually in evidence. He could present ingenious arguments even for his most outlandish ideas, which makes reading his writings unfailingly intriguing.

III

GÖDEL'S DOUBLE-EDGED COMPLETENESS PROOF

As was recounted in Chapter 1, Gödel's prepared presentation in Königsberg was a contributed paper that attracted little attention, even less than the announcement of his incompleteness result. As was also mentioned, this scheduled contribution was Gödel's completeness proof for ordinary first-order logic. Yet in a historical perspective— sometimes called wisdom by hindsight—this expected result has arguably affected the subsequent development of logic and the foundations of mathematics almost as profoundly as his unexpected incompleteness result. Gödel's friend Albert Einstein was once asked how he had reached his revolutionary insights. He answered, "By raising the questions that children are told not to ask." In his completeness paper, Gödel raised a question that had not been raised explicitly in print before and that many philosophers would still today like to discourage us from asking. Unfortunately he asked in such a way that to its (correct) answer was the expected one. This gave philosophers and logicians a false sense of security.

What Gödel proved was that the basic elementary part of logic known as ordinary first-order logic is complete. In order to understand what that means, one has to understand what is meant by first-order logic and what is meant by its completeness. Hence our first business is to come to know what first-order logic is.

This logic is a part of the logic which Frege as well as Russell and Whitehead had formulated. The first-order fragment was isolated for the first time in the lectures Hilbert gave in 1917-18 (with the assistance of Paul Bernays.) It was presented in print only in 1928 in the textbook *Grundzüge der theoretischen Logik* by Hilbert and Ackermann.

The nature of first-order languages can be understood painlessly by describing, not just these standardized languages as such, but the kind of subject matter that they can be used to deal with. As a semi-serious example of what a first-order language can be used for, we can consider a shared favorite pastime of the two sets of people among who logic took its longest strides in its historical development. This pastime is gossiping. It was eagerly practiced both by the ancient Athenians and by the famous group of intellectuals, most of them Cambridge University graduates, that is usually called the Bloomsbury group. The former society was the setting of the work of the founder of logic, Aristotle. The latter group the social context of the work of Bertrand Russell and A.N. Whitehead, the authors of the monumental *Principia Mathematica* (1911-1913) which is the first full-fledged (and consistent) codification of modern symbolic logic.

Now what kind of language do you need for gossiping? Your gossip must be about some set of people. Logicians call the generalized counterparts to these people *individuals* and the class formed by them *the universe of discourse.* (Frequently logicians speak of the domain of individuals rather than of the universe of discourse.) In our first-order language, we use as variables taking their values from the universe of discourse the lower case letters x, y, z, etc., possibly with subscripts, and as individual constants the lower case letters a, b, c, etc., again with subscripts if necessary. But above all we obviously need things to say about our individuals, that is to say, need *properties* to attribute to them and *relations* to hold between them. These two are expressed in a first-order language by what are called *predicates*. For instance, we might speak of properties like $M(x)$, $W(x)$, interpreted as "x is man", and "x is woman", respectively, and relations like $L(x, y)$

11

and C(x, y), to be read "x loves y" and "x is cleverer than y", respectively.

In some first-order languages we also need functions. If our domain of individuals is the set of natural numbers 0, 1, 2..., then the following function symbols might be included in the vocabulary of the first-order language in question:

$f(x,y) = z$ for $x + y = z$
$g(x,y) = z$ for $x \cdot y = z$
$h(x) = y$ for y is the successor to x

We must of course be able to combine our gossip-making statements with each other. This can be done by means of such propositional connectives as & (and), v (or), ~ (not), ⊃ (only if), and ↔ (if and only if). The technical name for these sentence formation operations are conjunction, disjunction, negation, conditional and equivalence. The fact that these translations of the formal language into English need certain further explanations need not bother us here. For instance, it must be realized that (A v B) expresses an inclusive disjunction like the Latin *vel* rather than the Latin *aut,* that is to say, it could be read "A or B or both".

We also want to express the perennial gambits people use to deflate gossip, such as "but everybody does that," and, "but someone else is also like that." Such retorts can be expressed by means of what are known as *quantifiers*. There are two of them. The *existential quantifier* (∃x) is to be interpreted as saying "for at least one member of the domain, call him (her, it) x, it is the case that" and the *universal quantifier* (∀x), is to be read "for each individual, call him (her, it) x, it is the case that." The remarkable fact here is that the admissible values of quantified variables are always individuals, and always comprise all individuals of the relevant universe of discourse. Of course, we must be able to express also quantification over some subset of the individuals, for instance over those individuals x that satisfy A(x). Such quantification is expressed in ordinary language by expressions like "some man" or "every woman" , in general "some A" or "every B". In our formal language they can be expressed by complete expressions like

(∃x) (A(x) & -----)   and
(∀x) (B(x) ⊃ -----)

We also need a symbol = for identity. Its negation can be written as ≠.

In the language so obtained, we can express all sorts of juicy gossip. Let us assume that we have the following names of (constants for) individuals (they are in fact names or nicknames of actual Bloomsbury characters):

> b = Bertie
> m = Maynard
> v = Virginia
> c = Carrington
> l = Lytton
> e = Leonard

Then the following statements will represent gossip (true or not) about those individuals:

(1) $(\forall x) (L(l, x) \supset M(x))$
(2) $(\forall x) (L(c, x) \supset c = l)$
(3) $L(v, e) \& L(e, v)$
(4) $(\exists x)(\exists y)(L(m, x) \& L(m,y) \& M(x) \& W(y))$
(5) $(\forall x) (L(b, x) \leftrightarrow {\sim}L(x, x))$
(6) $(\forall x) (M(b) \& ((M(x) \& (x \neq b)) \supset C(b, x)))$

A moment's thought will show you that (1) – (6) could be expressed in idiomatic English as follows:

(1)' Lytton loves only men
(2)' Carrington loves only Lytton
(3)' Virginia and Leonard love each other
(4)' Maynard loves both men and women [*i.e.* he loves some men and some women]
(5)' Bertie loves all and only those people who do not love themselves
(6)' Bertie is the cleverest of men

Once the reader internalizes this kind of first-order language, she or he can use it to express all sorts of scurrilous or non-scurrilous information.

Some people nevertheless prefer—at least in their professional role—to gossip about numbers rather than people. They are known as number theorists. One of them—actually, more a logician than a number theorist—has formulated an axiom system for elementary arithmetic (theory of natural numbers) known as Robinson arithmetic. The functions it employs are the three mentioned above. As the only constant we can use 0 (for zero).

The axioms of Robinson arithmetic are the following:

(A1)	$(\forall x)(\forall y)((h(x) = h(y)) \supset (x = y))$
(A2)	$(\forall x)(\sim(x = 0) \supset (\exists y)(x = h(y)))$
(A3)	$(\forall x) \sim(0 = h(x))$
(A4)	$(\forall x)(f(x,0) = x)$
(A5)	$(\forall x)(\forall y)(f(x,h(y)) = h(f(x,y))$
(A6)	$(\forall x)(g(x,0) = 0)$
(A7)	$(\forall x)(\forall y)(g(x,h(y)) = f(g(x,y),x)$

Here the basic symbols include an individual constant 0 and the functions f, g, h. If the constant 0 is interpreted as zero and the functions as addition, multiplication and succession, if addition and multiplication are written in the usual way and if the successor function is written as s(x), we obtain the following axiom system for arithmetic:

(A1)′	$(\forall x)(\forall y)((s(x) = s(y)) \supset (x = y))$
(A2)′	$(\forall x)(\sim(x \neq 0) \supset (\exists y)(x = s(y)))$
(A3)′	$(\forall x) \sim(0 = s(x))$
(A4)′	$(\forall x)(x + 0 = x)$
(A5)′	$(\forall x)(\forall y)((x + s(y)) = s(x + y))$
(A6)′	$(\forall x)(x \cdot 0 = 0)$
(A7)′	$(\forall x)(\forall y)((x \cdot s(y)) = ((x \cdot y) + x)))$

Here (A1)′ - (A7)′ can be taken as an axiom system of elementary arithmetic. They are easily seen to express truths about natural numbers. Other arithmetical truths can be derived from them by purely logical reasoning.

These explanations are nevertheless only a part of the story of first-order logic. They tell you what first-order languages are like, that is to say, languages whose logic is first-order logic. But what can we say of this logic itself? For this purpose, the reader is invited to have a closer look at the statement (5)′. It looks innocent enough. But there is one strange thing about it: it cannot be true. For if (5)′ is offered to you as an item of gossip, you can counter it with the question: But does Bertie love himself? If he does not, he is one of the poor people Bertie is said to love. If required to love himself, Bertie is one of the fortunate people not loved by Bertie. Both alternatives are impossible. Hence (5) and (5)' cannot possibly be true, no matter what the personal relationships in one's domain are or may be—and, indeed, independently of who Bertie and his *inamorata* are or may be.

The formal counterpart to this line of thought is to note that whatever is true of *every* is true of *each*. Hence what (5) says of everybody must be true of Bertie. In other words, if (5) is true, then so is

(7) $L(b,b) \leftrightarrow \sim L(b,b)$

But this is an obvious contradiction. Hence (5) cannot be true. This result does not depend in any way what relations L is or which individual b is. A sentence that is like (5) in that it cannot be true under any interpretation (in any "possible world"). Such sentences are said to be contradictory. Conversely, their negations are true under any interpretation or, as logicians could say, in every model of the language in question. Such sentences are called logical truths or (logically) valid sentences.

They are the propositions true under any interpretation of their symbols (other than logical ones). For instance, if in (5) the variables are stipulated to range over sets and $L(x,y)$ is interpreted as "x is a member of y," then (5) says that

(5)''   b is the set of all sets that are not members of themselves.

Early set theorists made assumptions that implied the existence of such a set. However, as Russell first pointed out, (5)'' is quite as much contradictory as (5) or (5)', and its negation as much of a logical truth as their negations.

A system of logic can now be said to be a method of mechanically listing a number of logically true sentences. Such a system of logic consists of a number of logical axioms and a number of rules of inference. The idea is that these rules of inference are completely mechanical, dependent only on the formal structure of the premises (inputs) of the inference. Hence the system can in principle be organized into an idealized computer. You program the axioms and the rules of inference into the computer which then will grind out more and more theorems obtainable from these axioms by these rules of inference. Sets of sentences (formulas) so obtainable are said to be recursively enumerable. The main idealization is that the "computer" in question has an infinite tape on which it can write symbols from a finite list of symbols. It is also assumed that the computer has no time limitations. Such idealized machines are known as Turing machines after the famous British logician and computer scientist Alan Turing (1912-1954).

If such a system of logic enumerates each and every logically true sentence of the language in which it is formulated, it is said to be *semantically complete.* Naturally it has to be required also that the system is *sound*, that is, that it enumerates only logically true formulas.

The same point can be made in slightly different terms. What precisely is it that Gödel proved about first-order logic? What is completeness? Logic is traditionally conceived of as a means of reaching certain conclusions, ideally proving them. In order to make sense of the completeness of a part of logic, we have to specify, first, precisely what that proof method is, in order to see how far it can reach. Second, we have to specify, independently of those proof methods, the extent they should reach in order to be complete. In brief, we have to establish both what logic (or a system of logic) actually can do and also what it ought to do.

Saying this already steps on many toes. Many a logical Protagoras will tell you that in logic our actual proof methods are the measure of all things. For instance, they claim that the meaning of logical constants like propositional connectives and quantifiers is determined by the rules of proof that govern them. If so, it would make no sense to speak of what our logic ought to do, which in their world implies that one cannot meaningfully speak of completeness in logic. One version of such views considers logic as the most general study of our actual world. As Bertrand Russell once put this point, logic deals with the real world quite as much as zoology, though with its more abstract aspects. Unless we do not have some a priori knowledge of those abstract objects, we cannot anticipate sight unseen what there is in the world of abstract objects, in other words, what ought to be possible to prove in logic.

In spite of this skepticism, there are several truly remarkable things about Gödel's result. The most fundamental one is perhaps the very conceptual distinction between what one can prove in a logic and what should be provable in it. What makes this feature remarkable is that the "should be" idea is what is called *model-theoretical* notion, not a *proof-theoretical* one. Completeness with respect to this "should be" means informally speaking that all logical truths of a certain part of logic can be formally proved. And logical truth is here a model-theoretical rather than proof-theoretical concept. Here the term "model theory", sometimes called instead "logical semantics" or "general model theory", deals with the relations of language to the reality it can represent. In contrast, "proof theory" refers to the study of formal proofs alone and "logical syntax" more generally to the study of the formal properties of some language. But what does it mean to think model-theoretically? If you are a model-theorist, you do not think of logic primarily as a vehicle of proof, but as a method of delineating a class of realizations or interpretations (logicians' "models") of a logical language, viz. those models in which a given sentence, for instance the conjunction of axioms, is true. In order to spell out this idea, we have to express the notions of model and truth. This task was accomplished around the same time as Gödel's famous early results by Alfred Tarski, whose work thus helped to put Gödel's results in a wider perspective. In particular Tarski showed how to define truth in a model of a first-order language. All this can be done by using a richer metalanguage without any reference to the rules of proof.

The problem of the completeness of first-order logic now becomes the question whether the formal methods of proof exhaust the class of logical truths (truths in every model). Even though questions concerning completeness can be traced back to Hilbert's project, it is a major achievement on Gödel's part to have recognized the nature of the completeness problem, which amounts essentially to a distinction between model-theoretical concepts (like logical truth, aka truth in every model) and proof-theoretical notions, such as formal provability. Indeed, model-theoretical questions are the Gödelian counterpart to questions that only children and Albert Einstein spontaneously ask.

At the same time, Gödel's actual completeness result had, historically speaking, the effect of minimizing the distinction between model-theoretical and proof-theoretical concepts. For what he showed was that the class of logical truths of the received first-order logic can be captured by purely synthetical proof methods. In other words, after having introduced the crucial distinction between model-theoretical notions, at least in the special case of first-order logical truth vs. formal provability in first-order logic, Godel showed that in this case distinction makes no difference. I suspect that this aspect of Gödel's result has had the effect of discouraging philosophers' and logicians' interest in model theory, or at least discouraged them from believing in the foundational and philosophical significance of model theory. What is usually called "model theory" is, in fact, a relatively specialized discipline founded by Tarski and his associates beginning in the late

17

fifties. Tarski himself did not believe that in this way we can achieve major insights into the logic of ordinary language.

Gödel's completeness proof for the ordinary first-order logic thus, in effect, served to reassure logicians and philosophers that they could happily go on practicing their proof-theoretical problems. Alas, this sense of security has turned out to be a false one. One way in which this guilty secret has been betrayed is the discovery that the received first-order logic that Gödel's completeness proof deals with is not the full unrestricted logic of quantifiers it has been advertised as being. Gödel's completeness proof is therefore unrepresentative of the conceptual situation in logic in general. His Einsteinian question, the question concerning semantical completeness, was asked about a wrong logic.

This statement might be found surprising and even objectionable in many quarters. The received first-order logic is generally considered as *the* basic logic of ours, at the very least as *the* logic of quantifiers. When I once expressed doubts of the status of the ordinary first-order logic as a faithful representation of the logic of ordinary language to a senior philosopher of language, he looked at me with an expression of mock shock and exclaimed, "Nothing is sacred in philosophy any longer." Yet it can be shown that the so-called ordinary first-order logic is not the full unrestricted logic of first-order quantifiers, that is, of quantifiers ranging over individuals as distinguished from high-order entities. I will return to the question as to how this surprising development is related to Gödel's ideas.

IV

GÖDEL'S BACKGROUND

In order to understand the impact of Gödel's work and its results, a brief sketch of his background is in order. The development of the foundations of mathematics in the nineteenth century is often described by speaking of a quest of rigour and strictness. This is not the most important part of the story, however. On of the most significant novelties of nineteenth century mathematics was the increasing use of mathematical and logical tools for conceptual analysis. For instance, in the theory of surfaces developed by Gauss and Rieman such pretheoretical geometrical notions as curvature were analyzed in terms of the concepts of differential calculus. For another example, work in the foundations of analysis led in the hands of mathematicians like Karl Weierstrass to definitions of such basic concepts of analysis as continuity, convergence, differentiation, etc. These definitions did not appeal to our pretheoretical ideas about continuity, infinity, or infinitely small, but were in terms of numbers and logic. Because of this ontological economy, the work done in this tradition helped to eliminate many confusions and puzzles associated with "infinitesimal" analysis. Much of the logic used in the enterprise nevertheless remained merely informal. When it was later analyzed, it turned out to be mostly of the first-order variety explained in the preceding chapter.

This development in a sense culminated in the largely parallel work by such mathematicians as Georg Cantor, Gottlob Frege and Richard Dedekind. Cantor developed what is known as set theory, that is the study of sets and classes of any kind, especially infinite sets of different varieties. Surprisingly, it turned out that infinity is not a simple concept, in the sense that there are hierarchies of infinite sets of different magnitudes, technically known as cardinalities. For instance, the cardinality $\aleph_0$ of the set of natural numbers is expectedly smallest infinite number. Furthermore, Cantor showed that for any given set of cardinality α, the set of all its subsets has the cardinality 2^α which is greater than α.

Questions concerning infinite cardinalities are sometimes very difficult. For instance, the apparently simple question whether there are cardinalities between $\aleph_0$ and $2^{\aleph_0}$ still without an answer. This famous question is known as the *continuum problem* and the answer that there are none is called the (special) continuum hypothesis. The more general question whether there can be cardinalities β between any α and 2^α is known as the general continuum problem.

In spite of such unsolved problems, in some size, shape or form set theory has often been considered and—is still frequently considered—as the true foundation of mathematics.

At the same time, Frege developed for the first time an explicit logic by means of which such conceptual analyses could be carried out. Often, these analyses took the form of a reduction. For instance, Dedekind showed how the theory of real numbers could be construed as a part of the theory of infinite sets of rational numbers. Rational numbers can in be thought of as pairs of integers. Thus to speak of the rational number, a/b, where a and b do not have any factors in common, is simply to speak of the ordered pair <a, b>.

Frege took an even bolder step and tried to define natural numbers in purely logical terms. If successful, this would have meant a reduction of entire mathematics—with the possible exception of geometry—to logic. The claim that such a reduction is possible is known as the logicist thesis. But for such a task, the (ordinary) first-order logic described in the preceding chapter is not enough. For instance, Frege defined his concept of number by using the notion of equicardinality of two sets A and B. By this fancy term, logicians merely mean that A and B have the same number of members. Accordingly the logic Frege developed was in effect a higher-order logic.

20

But what is meant by higher-order logic? A simple answer can be given by reference to the first-order logic explained in Chapter 3. In it, all the values of quantified variables are individuals—the subjects, so to speak, that are being gossiped about. In other words, by "all" and "some" we always mean in first-order logic "all *individuals*" and "some *individuals*". We jump to second-order logic when we begin to quantify over classes, properties, relations and/or functions of individuals. We might even resort to such second-order quantification in our actual gossip. I can imagine Bloomsberries saying to each other things like "Bertie has some redeeming qualities," "I don't see what adorable features Carrington sees in Lytton," "There are at least six clubs Clive belongs to," or "I wonder what kind of relationship there is between Maynard and Vanessa." We move from second-order to third-order language when we begin to quantify over properties and relations of properties and relations, and so on.

Such higher-order quantification can be understood in two different ways. In first-order logic, the two basic quantifiers are not only individualistic but also totally democratic. They always range over all the individuals in one's universe of discourse. For instance, in doing number theory, $(\exists x)$ means "for some number, call it x, it is true that". Here x can be any number. But what precisely can be meant by higher-order quantification? Such quantification is intrinsically ambiguous. If I speak of all sets of natural numbers, my words can be taken in two different ways. If my name is Frank Ramsay, I presumably intend to be understood to mean all possible set whose members are individuals, no matter whether I can name them one by one or define the totality they form. But if my name is Bertrand Russell, I am likely to be taken to speak of all classes of numbers that can be defined or otherwise picked out by some characteristic or other. These two kinds of interpretation are sometimes called the standard and nonstandard interpretations respectively, but this terminology may itself be somewhat nonstandard. The distinction itself, even though it has played an extremely important subterranean role in the development of the foundations of mathematics, has to this day remained something of a professional secret. In the following, by "second-order logic" or "higher-order logic," I will normally mean a logic with standard interpretation.

Higher-order logic with standard interpretation is stronger than first-order logic. This strength should be welcomed by mathematics and philosophers, for first-order logic is not strong enough to serve as the proper foundation of mathematics, the daydreams of some logicists notwithstanding. For instance, you cannot express in an ordinary first-order language the fact that two classes, say the classes of those individuals that satisfy A(x) and B(x), have the same number of individuals. Yet it is easily expressed in second-order terms (assuming standard interpretation), for instance as follows:

(1) $(\exists f)(\exists g)(\forall x)(\forall y)((A(x) \supset B(f(x))) \& (B(y) \supset A(g(y))) \& (x = g(y) \leftrightarrow (y = f(x))))$

A moment's thought shows you that this expression really captures the equicardinality. For instance, you can note that the functions f and g are inverses of each other. Once you see this, you can see from the first two clauses that f maps the sets of individuals satisfying A(x) and B(x) on each other one-to-one, i.e. have the same number of members. Likewise, the important principle known as the axiom of choice cannot be formulated in first-order logic but can be formulated in second-order terms as the axiom schema.

(2) $(\forall x)(\exists y) S[x, y] \supset (\exists f)(\forall x) S[x,f(x)]$

It might therefore seem tempting to base one's mathematical theories on second-order or higher-order logic rather than on the ordinary first-order logic. This is what Frege as well as Russell and Whitehead were trying to do. But such an approach is not in fashion in our days for historical reasons that have a lot to do with Gödel's work, at least indirectly. For one thing, higher-order logic is semantically incomplete. This can be seen from Gödel's first incompleteness theorem as follows: In second-order logic, it is easy to formulate an axiom system for elementary arithmetic which has only one model (up to isomorphism). All we need to do is essentially to add to the axiom of a suitable first-order number theory a second-order induction axiom, for instance

(3) $(\forall X) ((X(0) \& ((\forall z)(X(z) \supset X(s(z)))) \supset (\forall z)X(z))$

If the underlying logic were semantically complete, that is, if every logical consequence of the second-order axiom system were formally provable, we would have a method of formally proving every truth of elementary arithmetic in violation of Gödel's first incompleteness theorem.

But now the reader may be totally confused. How can second-order logic be more powerful than first-order logic and capable of doing more for the foundations of mathematics if it is itself incomplete?

22

I suspect that if the reader is confused, he or she is in large company. There exists a widespread confusion or at least unclarity concerning the very idea of completeness. A few definitions and explanations might therefore be in order here.

Because of the incompleteness of high-order logic, it becomes an urgent question as to what assumptions a mathematician can make about it. Frege worked on the basis of one set of such assumptions for decades, with little encouragement or appreciation. In 1903 he nevertheless seemed to have completed his life's work, summed up in a monumental two-volume work *Grundgesetze der Arithmetik* (*Fundamental Laws of Arithmetic*). Just when he was reading the proofs of the second volume, he received a letter from a young English logician-philosopher named Bertrand Russell. Russell pointed out that there was a contradiction in Frege's basic assumptions. They implied the existence of the set of all (and only) those sets that were not members of themselves. Yet, as was pointed out in Chapter 3, such a set cannot exist.

The contradiction Russell pointed out turned out to be extremely difficult to exorcise from Frege's higher-order logic without destroying its usefulness for the purposes Frege wanted to use it. What is more, similar problems turned up in the foundations of set theory. The resulting uncertainty was felt keenly not only by philosophers of mathematics and logicians but even by mathematicians concerned. One reason was that the uncertainty concerning the foundations of set theory affected the modes of reasoning used by mathematicians in their own work. For instance, if you are given an infinite set of nonempty sets, can you always assume that there is a function that picks out from each set precisely one member? The assumption that you can is known as the axiom of choice, and it has been viewed with suspicion with some mathematicians and philosophers.

This uncertainty affected deeply people's entire way of thinking about the foundations of mathematics in the early years of the twentieth century. People spoke generally of a "crisis of the foundations" (*Grundlagenkrisis*) of mathematics.

Of the responses to this "crisis of the foundations," two are especially relevant here. One of them is, in effect, to restrict logic to first-order logic. But how can you then deal with the set? The answer set theorists give is as simple as it is dubious. Sets are thought of as individuals of sorts. The theory of sets is then formulated in the same way as any first order axiomatic theory, known as axiomatic set theory. The principles of reasoning that go beyond first-order logic will then have to be captured—if possible—in the form of first-order axioms or axiom schemes for this first-order of choice has to be formulated as a first-order theory. The only primitive nonlogical concept of this theory is the membership relation, usually expressed by $\in$. For instance, the axiom of choice has to be formulated as a first-order axiom or axiom schema.

Axiomatic treatment of set theory was started by Ernest Zermelo in 1903. It is now enjoying a virtual monopoly as an approach to set theory. It is not without its problems, however, some of which we will meet later.

For one thing, doing everything set-theoretically leaves the nature and the laws of higher-order logic in obscurity. For instance, is the axiom of choice merely a principle concerning the nature of sets, or is a logical principle? A version of the axiom of choice can in fact be formulated as a truth of second-order logic:

(4) $(\forall x)(\exists y) S[x, y] \supset (\exists f)(\forall x) S[x, f(x)]$

Here the set of sets mentioned in the original formulation of the axiom of choice has as its members all the classes of individuals y satisfying S[a, y] for some constant individual a. Far from considering the axiom of choice as an optional set-theoretical assumption, Hilbert went so far as to express the hope that future developments in the foundations of mathematics will make it as obviously true as $2+2 = 4$

For a while, another response to the *Grundlagenkrisis* was even more prominent philosophically. That was the approach to the foundations of mathematics by the great German mathematician David Hilbert. The motivation of his approach has been generally misunderstood, however. Hilbert was first and foremost a representative of the axiomatic method. Any mathematical theory and Hilbert believed any sufficiently advanced scientific theory ought to be formulated in the form of an axiomatic theory where all substantial assumptions are formulated as explicit axioms. All the other truths of the theory in question should then be theorems of the axiom system in question, that is to say, logical consequences of the axioms. If the logic that is being used is semantically complete, then all these theorems can be derived by explicit formal rules of logical inference from the axioms. These theorems are the truths in all the models (i.e. under all the different interpretations) of the axiom system. Thus as soon as a given axiom system has models, deriving theorems from it is a meaningful enterprise. Even axiom systems that might at first sight seem unnatural, not to say perverse, like the axiom systems for non-Euclidean geometry, might turn out to have realizations that are

24

eminently worth studying systematically.

But all this is predicated on the assumption that the given axiom system has at least one model, in other words that it is not inconsistent (self-contradictory). How can we know that? Can we know that this or that first-order axiom system for set theory is not inconsistent? Frege's example shows how difficult it sometimes is to know such a thing. Do we really *know* that even our arithmetic is consistent? Sometimes we can prove the consistency of an axiom system relative to another by interpreting it in terms of the latter. For instance, Felix Klein was able to prove the consistency of a certain non-Euclidean system of geometry by interpreting it in the Euclidean geometry. Other non-Euclidean plane geometries can be interpreted as geometries that would be true on the surface of a sphere or of a hyperbolic surface. Here spheres and hyperboloids must of course be specified by perfectly Euclidean methods—or so it seems. But at the very foundations of mathematics, there is nothing more fundamental that could be used as the target of a re-interpretation.

What Hilbert did was to try to prove the consistency of different axiom systems in the sense of their having models in a new way. Instead of considering models and their interpretability in each other, Hilbert considered what can be proved in a formal system of geometry. If it can be proved that one cannot derive an inconsistency from the axioms by the formal rules of logic, and if the logic used is semantically complete, then the axiom system is consistent in the strong sense of having models in which all the axioms are true.

This is an ingenious idea, inspired by Hilbert's realization that the logical derivation of theorems from axiom is independent of the interpretation of non-logical concepts used in the axiom system. As Hilbert once put it in his flamboyant way, a valid derivation of a geometrical theorem from geometrical axioms remains valid if instead of points, lines and circles we speak in the axioms of tables, chairs and beermugs. Hilbert's working hypothesis was that it was easier to prove consistency in the sense of nonderivability of a formal contradiction than the construction of a model in which all the axioms are true.

This project has come to be known as Hilbert's Program. It dominated the discussions about the foundations of mathematics in the twenties. Hilbert's program is predicated on certain assumptions, however, over and above the purely formal character of the logical consequence relations that take us from the axioms to the theorems. The most important of them is the semantical completeness (at least a partial one) of the logic that is being used. In order to see this, recall that Hilbert was trying to show the model-theoretical consistency of axiom systems, in the sense of their having models (interpretations making all the axioms true), by showing their proof-theoretical (deductive) consistency, in other words, by showing that no contradiction can be formally derived from them by means of the underlying logic L. But the existence of models follows at once from the deductive consistency only if the logic L that is being used is semantically complete. As was explained above, such semantical completeness means that whatever is logically valid that is to say, true in all models, can actually be proved by means of the logic in question. Hence if a logic is not semantically complete, there may be sentences that are not true in any model but whose negations are not provable. An axiom system which is deductively consistent but without any models would be case in point. One can think of such an axiom system as implying an inconsistency which prevents it form having any models but which is so deeply hidden that the incomplete logic cannot bring it out to the open.

Of course, to carry out a Hilbert-style consistency proof from some particular theory, say elementary arithmetic, one does not need to assume the semantical completeness of the underlying logic *tout court* but only as far as the consequences of that particular theory are concerned. However, no one seems to have been concerned with the possibility of such conditional completeness, largely because logicians and mathematicians took the completeness of their logic for granted. Hilbert's entire program was tacitly predicated on the semantical completeness of the logic he was using. Now this logic was the ordinary first-order logic described in Chapter 2. And its completeness was the very thing Gödel proved in his completeness theorem.

Thus, it is fair to say that Gödel's first main result, his completeness theorem for ordinary first-order logic, is intimately related to Hilbert's program. It shows that the main presupposition of Hilbert's entire enterprise is in fact satisfied. Even though this was what everybody expected, it is a remarkable achievement. Systematically speaking, the semantical completeness of the underlying logic ought to have been shown before the Hilbert's program was launched. But instead proving it, Hilbert and his associates had simply assumed it. Gödel came to their rescue in the nick of time.

At the same time, by formulating the completeness question for first-order logic, Gödel was sowing the seeds of doubt or at the very least the seeds of possible alternative answers. By beginning to distinguish model-theoretical and proof-theoretical concepts from each other Gödel launched a line of thought that is potentially disruptive to the happy coexistence of the two kinds of notions. This distinction was forced on Gödel and on the world by his incompleteness results.

V

GÖDEL'S PUZZLING INCOMPLETENESS PROOF

Gödel's completeness proof was initially thought of as unsurprising. In contrast, his incompleteness theorem was experienced by most mathematicians, logicians and philosophers as a surprise. The lack of response in Königsberg was due to the novelty of Gödel's and perhaps even more to the novelty of the questions he was asking. Once it was understood what his answers were, people realized that something remarkable had happened.

But what precisely is the mysterious incompleteness theorem that Gödel proved – and how did he prove it? There are in logic and mathematics baffling theorems and lines of proof. Yet Gödel's first incompleteness result seems stranger than others by an order of magnitude. There had been impossibility results in mathematics before. It had for instance been proved that you cannot trisect an angle by any

Gödel's Puzzling Incompleteness Proof

uniform method with only ruler and compass and that you cannot solve general equations of the fifth degree or higher algebraically. But what Gödel claimed to have proven was that there are in any first-order axiom system of arithmetic—that is, in an axiom system like the Robinson arithmetic presented in Chapter 3 above—there are arithmetical propositions which are true but which cannot be proved logically in that system. The only assumption Gödel had to make is that the axiom system is not formally inconsistent, that is, that a contradiction cannot be derived from it by means of the explicit rules of logical proof. How can Gödel prove that his crucial proposition is not logically provable by using the very same logic? And how can he know that the proposition in question is true if he cannot prove it?

There have been lots of strange reactions, not only to Gödel's result, but to the proof he gave for it. Not to put too fine a point on it, several more or less respectable philosophers, mathematicians and computer scientists have made fools of themselves over Gödel's proof. A few mathematicians even maintain that Gödel's argument has a technical flaw. One distinguished legal scholar mistakenly claimed to have pointed out a fallacy in the argument. A philosopher who rushed to Gödel's defense turned out to have partly misunderstood Gödel's result himself. In our days, the well-known computer scientist Gregory Chaitin has claimed to have found a connection between Gödel's result and the information content of arithmetical axiom systems. Unfortunately for Chaitin, his information measures have turned out not to measure anything that could conceivably be called information. Clearly there is a need of understanding clearly what Gödel did and did not prove – and precisely how he did it.

More abstractly speaking, the idea of applying a language to itself, for instance for the purpose of proving that something cannot be logically proved, seemed dubious to many logicians and philosophers. The most serious objections focused on trying to speak of the meaning and truth of the expressions of a language in the same language. But to this particular objection Gödel would have had an answer. At least initially, it sufficed for him to speak in his logical language only of the purely formal or, as the usual term goes, purely syntactical features of his arithmetical language. Gödel's way of doing so was not entirely novel, but it is nevertheless not unfair that his particular way of making an arithmetical language to speak of its own formalism has since become known as the technique of Gödel numbering. In spite of the simplicity of his basic idea, understanding the notion of Gödel numbering takes you a long way towards understanding Gödel's famous proof. A brief sketch of the method of Gödel numbering is therefore in order.

We can assume that some formal system of elementary arithmetic is given, for instance the Robinson arithmetic of Chapter 4, together with a set of formal rules of proof. Then it helps to make first certain inessential simplifications. Several of the symbols of the arithmetical language of Chapter 4 can be dispensed with. Indeed, we can replace $(\exists x)$ by $\sim(\forall x)\sim$, $(A \lor B)$ by $\sim(\sim A$ & $\sim B)$, $(A \supset B)$ by $\sim(\sim A$ & $\sim B)$, $(A \leftrightarrow B)$ by $((A$ & $B) \lor (\sim A$ & $\sim B))$ and the sequence of variables x, y, z, $\cdots$ by x', x'', x''', ... Conjunction sign & can be dispensed with by writing $(A$ & $B)$ as $(A) (B)$, and the universal quantifier can be written (x) instead of $(\forall x)$.

Then we need only the following symbols: $+$, $\cdot$, s, $=$, $\forall$, &, $\sim$, 0, x, $'$, (,)

But these symbols are purely conventional. Arithmetic is presumably a free country, and even if it is not, there is not law against renaming those symbols. For instance, we can replace them by the numbers 9, 8, 7, 6, 5, 4, 3, 2, 1, 0. The correlation of the two alternative sets of symbols will then be the following:

+	·	s	=	~	0	x	'	(	)
9	8	7	6	5	4	3	2	1	0

Then every sequence of symbols corresponds to a definite natural number, its Gödel number. In particular, every well-formed sentence S corresponds to a number g(S), known as the Gödel number of S. For instance, the first two axioms of the Robinson arithmetic can be written in the abbreviated notation as

(A.1)″ $(x)(x') \sim ((s(x) = s(x'))(\sim (x = x')))$
(A.2)″ $((x)\sim((\sim(x = 0))((x')\sim(x = s(x'))))$

Hence their Gödel numbers are respectively

(A.1)‴   1301320511713067132001513632000
(A.2)‴   113051151364001132051367320000

The reader may (or may not) want to amuse himself or herself by writing out the Gödel numbers of the other axioms of Robinson arithmetic. If the idea of Gödel numbering is still felt strange by the reader, one thing I can do is to think of them as the Social Security numbers of arithmetical formulas. Another reassuring analogy may be to cryptography, where verbal messages are routinely coded into sequences of numbers. Furthermore, all the operations on formulas involved in logical inferences become arithmetical operations on their Gödel numbers. I am not going to prove this fact, not because it is difficult but because it takes more space (and more patience) than I have available to me at this moment. However, this fact is not hard to believe. For instance, if a Gödel number of a sentence is of the form:

(1) 1g(A) 01g(B)0

then it is clearly the Gödel number of (A) (B), i.e. of

(2) (A & B)

Hence to infer B from (2) corresponds to moving from (1) to g(B), which is clearly an arithmetical operation.

The most important upshot of this development is that there exists an arithmetical predicate Pr[x] such that it applies to the Gödel number x = g(A) of a sentence A if and only if A is provable in the axiomatized system of arithmetic. It is obvious that Pr[x] will be a highly complex predicate. It is almost equally obvious, I trust, that there are no obstacles to actually constructing one, even though it takes a heroic effort to do so. Indeed, to have constructed such a predicate was the first main result that was required for Gödel's proof.

It may be useful to pause here and think of what is involved in Gödel numbering. As a purely formal technique, it is not hard to understand. But when one looks at numbers and arithmetical statements after the numbering has been carried out, one's head may begin to spin. What do arithmetical propositions now say? Do they speak of numbers or numerical formulas? Are Gödel numbers really numbers or are they merely formulas in disguise? Fortunately there is an analogy that can help one to grasp the situation. To use the technique of Gödel numbering is like staging an amateur play. The actors have their normal life outside the play, but they also have a role in the tragedy or perhaps the farce in question. As a consequence, what one of them says can typically be taken in two different ways, either as it would be understood in his or her everyday life outside the play or else as a line in the play. Likewise, one and the same arithmetical proposition can now be taken in two different ways, either as a proposition about numbers in their everyday life as numbers, or as a statement about the formulas that those same numbers represent when they play different characters in their Gödelian play. In neither case, neither in a stage play nor in a metamathematician's skit, need there be any real danger of confusion. Indeed, understanding the technique of Gödel numbering thus need not cause any greater difficulties than understanding playacting. You can take any arithmetical statement to be about numbers in their everyday life as odd or even numbers, prime numbers or factors of other numbers, and so on. But you can, if you want, to follow Stanislavski's and Gödel's example and stage a skit in which numbers play the role of arithmetical formulas. This does not eliminate the possibility of taking what they express in the prosaic everyday arithmetical sense. However, in the logical drama staged by Gödel, this is not the way we are supposed to view them. For a while, we are asked to suspend our realistic attitude and view our friends and neighbors among numbers as if they were acting an artificial role in a logician's play. Such a *double-entendre* use of arithmetic requires a certain sophistication, but there is nothing paradoxical or even puzzling about it, any more than about watching a play.

Moreover, just as in the same way as in a play the actors and actresses normally speak the same language as they speak in ordinary life, with the same literal meanings and the same logic, just in the same way the same logic applies to arithmetical statements on either way of construing them. The same statements are of course logically true no matter whether we are speaking of numbers or formulas. The difference in both cases is that this common language can be given two different interpretations, relative to two different classes of individuals (ordinary folk vs. characters in a drama or ordinary numbers vs. numbers as codifications of formulas). This implies that the same statements are logically true in the two cases, for it was seen that logical truths are precisely the truths that are independent of the interpretations of the language in question.

This analogy can be given a further twist. Sometimes in a contemporary movie or television episode a public figure is given a cameo role as playing himself or herself. For instance, I remember seeing an old movie about an imaginary tennis champion in which John McEnroe and Pancho Gonzales played themselves, and a television episode in which Mike Ditka had the role of Mike Ditka when he was still the coach of the Chicago Bears. In such a situation, the self-depicting actor's words must be referred to the same person also in his metier outside the play. This is relatively rare in a thespian setting but there is nothing paradoxical about it. Now what Gödel showed that a similar coincidence between a play and the reality can materialize in the realm of numbers.

Indeed, this coincidence happens routinely. The result that shows this is known as the diagonal lemma. What it says is the following:

For any formula F[x] of elementary number theory with precisely one free variable x, there is a number n which is the Gödel number of the formula F[n], that is to say, of the formula obtained from F[x] by replacing the variable x by the numeral n that represents n. (In the symbolism envisaged here, n would of course be

(3) s(s(s(...s(s(0))...)))   (n occurrences of s)

What this means intuitively is that the number n is taken in its play-acting role as representing a certain statement. When this statement is unpacked, it turns out to say that the statement number n has a certain property. In other words, in its play-acting role n says "I have the property P[x]," where the "I" in question happens to be the off-stage person, pardon me, the off-stage number that on the stage plays the role of n. It is thus as if John McEnroe would make a statement about John McEnroe the real person while playing himself in a movie.

From the diagonal lemma together with the representability of Pr[x], Gödel's first incompleteness theorem follows. For when the diagonal lemma is applied to the formula

(4) ~Pr[x]

we obtain a number g such that it is the Gödel number of

(5) ~Pr[g]

Now what does (5) say? It says that the formula with the Gödel number g is not provable. But that formula is (5) itself. Hence if (5) were provable, then its negation would also be provable, and the system would be inconsistent. But Gödel assumed that the system of arithmetic he was using is consistent. If so, (5) is not provable in it. But this is precisely what it says itself, wherefore it is true but not provable, just as Gödel's result claims.

It is of some importance that this argument does not prove the truth of ~Pr[g] absolutely, only on the assumption that the axiom system of arithmetic that is being used is consistent. Several different explanations are needed here. What was just sketched differs in one important respect from Gödel's own exposition. Gödel did not formulate explicit the diagonal lemma, even though it has been suggested that it is implicit in his work. He proved directly the existence of the self-referential Gödel number for the predicate ~Pr[x]. The diagonal lemma nevertheless shows more clearly what is involved here.

In explaining the play analogy, I said that in a Gödelian context many arithmetical statements can be taken in two different ways, either as normal arithmetical statements or else as lines in a Gödelian play. If you recall this, you will realize that I have used both in the diagonal lemma and in the critical Gödelian sentence (5) the "playacting" sense. This is perfectly in order and does not in the least reflect on their significance. However, we must keep in mind that they can also be read in a different way, that is to say, as routine number-theoretical statements.

Here the play analogy helps us to appreciate the significance of Gödel's argument. If we think of this argument in terms of numerically codified propositions, his argument (which leads from the assumption of the consistency axiomatization of arithmetic to the existence of an unprovable sentence) may very well prompt puzzlement. There exists in fact an extensive literature among philosophers discussing the proof methods which Gödel used or which can be used to prove the diagonal lemma. This literature is nevertheless an exercise in futility. For the logical validity of the argument under one interpretation is the same as on another. And on the number-theoretical (i.e., non-play-acting) interpretation this argument is, ingenious, but nothing but an elementary arithmetical argument.

In other words, as plain vanilla number-theoretical statements, the diagonal lemma and crucial Gödelian sentence (5) are not only unproblematically true but unproblematically provable. As Gödel himself emphasized, they are on a par philosophically with any old theorem or metatheorem of elementary arithmetic. They reveal certain fascinating things about arithmetic. They might prompt you to wonder about the surprising versatility of as basic a part of mathematics as number theory, which turns out to be able to reproduce its own structure within itself. If you want to understand the nature of arithmetic, you have to understand these results. But it is absolutely crucial to realize that the significance of these arithmetical results pertains to mathematics, not to logic or to the limitations of logic—or to any other philosophical problem whatsoever. The diagonal lemma deals with any property of arithmetical propositions that can be captured in elementary arithmetic. It does not deal with unprovability any more than with being the Gödel number of a provable proposition, true proposition or unknown proposition.

As an exercise illustrating this point, the reader might want to use the diagonal lemma to prove that the property of being (the Gödel number of) a true arithmetical proposition cannot be expressed in a formal system of elementary arithmetic.

What follows? We are now in position to see that any particular proof given to Gödel's first incompleteness theorem is philosophically irrelevant. To inquire into the methods used to prove the diagonal lemma or the proposition (5) is an important exercise in the philosophical analysis of arithmetic. But it has no philosophical significance whatsoever. It does not, because it cannot, show anything about the reasons why elementary arithmetic is incomplete. The philosophers who have discussed *ad nauseam* the methods Gödel used in his argument are barking up the wrong proof. This fact was initially obscured to some extent by Gödel's proving (5) directly and not formulating it as a corollary to the diagonal lemma, for it is the generality of the diagonal lemma that shows the irrelevance of the details Gödel's proof to special problem of incompleteness. But later philosophers do not have this excuse.

For instance, Wittgenstein's well-known comments on Gödel's proof are interesting in that they throw light on his way of thinking and perhaps indirectly on the philosophy of mathematics in general. However, as Gödel himself quickly saw, they have no relevance whatsoever to the nature of Gödel's incompleteness result.

At bottom, what is involved here is nothing stranger than the fact that actors playing their roles can speak the same language as they do in their private lives, with precisely the same logical truths.

Gödel himself sought to illustrate his argument by comparing it with the famous (or infamous) paradox of the liar. There is in fact a certain partial similarity between the liar paradox and Gödel's argument. Suppose I write:

(6)   This statement is false.

Then if (6) is true, it is false, and if it is false, then it is true—not unlike the Gödelian proposition. Moreover, the self-referential word "this" is not essential. I could equally well write:

(7)   The displayed sentence (7) of Chapter 5 of the book *Gödel* by

Jaakko Hintikka is false.

Now attempts have been made to explain the import of the sentence.

(8) ~Tr[g]

by suggesting that what it says is, "I am false." Such an explanation of Gödel's first incompleteness theorem by reference illuminating in some ways, especially heuristically, but it is seriously incomplete as an account of what happens with the puzzling Gödelian sentence and therefore creates unnecessary puzzles. As Gödel's very first announcement of his result (quoted above in Chapter 1) shows, the whole point of the theorem is to produce a dyed-in-the-wool arithmetical statement which is on a par with such propositions as number theorists typically deal with, for instance Fermat's or Goldbach's theorems, and which is true but unprovable. In contrast, the liar sentence does not speak of numbers at all but of propositions like itself. How can the unprovability of the Gödelian sentence therefore be explainable by a comparison with the behavior of the liar sentence?

The answer is that it cannot. The secret of the Gödel sentence is not that it is self-referential but that it is like a statement made in a play about real people. The real logic of the Gödel sentence is not comparable with the logic of the statement made in a play. Suppose that Clint Eastwood says, playing a role in a movie, "In this situation, even Clint Eastwood could not keep a straight face." This statement is part of the movie, not of real life. Yet the meaning and the truth of that statement have to be judged by reference to real persons, in this case Clint Eastwood the actor. Its truth of falsity can only be decided by examining when the actual man would smile in a certain situation, not when a character in a movie might grin. Likewise the Gödelian sentence is a part of a self-referential play. In spite of it, truth and provability have to be judged as if it were a run-of-the-mill arithmetical statement—which it of course is.

To sum up, it is often said that Gödel's argument involves self-referential statements. This a half-truth, however. The number figuring in a Gödelian statement does refer to itself, but only as playing a different role from the one in which the statement is made.

The unproblematic character of Gödel's proof is reflected by the fact that it can be expressed—as von Neumann quickly saw—in the very same system of arithmetic it pertains to. Because of this, it follows that if the consistency of a system of elementary arithmetic were provable in the same arithmetic, so were also the Gödelian sentence (5), that is, ~Pr[g]. Since (5) is not provable (if the system is consistent), the consistency of a consistent system of elementary arithmetic cannot be proved in the same arithmetic. This result is known, as was noted in Chapter 1, as Gödel's second incompleteness theorem.

It is nevertheless dangerous to speak simply of "assuming the consistency" of some particular formulation of elementary arithmetic. Solomon Feferman has shown that there are senses of consistency in which the consistency of elementary arithmetic is probable arithmetically. Hence Gödel's second incompleteness theorem cannot be considered merely as a trivial consequence of the first theorem. The matter of consistency proofs is therefore not closed by Gödel's results.

The outline that has been presented of Gödel's impossibility theorem shows certain important things about it. First and foremost, the construction Gödel uses to find an unprovable proposition G is relative to some given axiom system of arithmetic. What the conclusion says is that G is unprovable in the given system and yet true. The same proposition can be provable in another sound axiom system of arithmetic. (By soundness one means that all the theorems provable in the axiom system in question are true.) Indeed, merely by adding G to the axioms of the given system we can construct such a system.

Hence Gödel's impossibility theorem does not show that there are any true but absolutely unprovable propositions in arithmetic or anywhere else. What is shows is that not all true arithmetical propositions can be proved mechanically, in one and the same formal system. Even in as simple a branch of mathematics as elementary arithmetic, mathematicians not only must find proofs of new theorems from old axioms; they also have to search for ever more and more powerful (but true) axioms.

For instance, what is provable in the Robinson arithmetic does not exhaust all arithmetical truths. Part of the job description of a number theorist is therefore the search for such stronger axioms.

Gödel would have agreed with this conclusion. He did not offer any examples of true arithmetical propositions of authentic mathematical interest not probable in the usual systems of elementary arithmetic. Others have done to, however. The most interesting examples of arithmetical propositions not provable in the usual axiomatizations have been discovered by Paris and Harrington.

VI

THE CONSEQUENCES OF INCOMPLETENESS

The history of logical theory in the last century and a half could be written as a mystery story full of sharp twists of the plot. The way in which I have written the early Gödel chapters of the story, it is like a detective story in the sense that there are plenty of clues which should—or at least might—enable the reader to predict what will happen next.

One of the clues is the dominating role of Hilbert's metamathematical project on the scene of the foundations of metamathematics around 1930. Because of this role, the first thing mathematicians and philosophers paid attention in Gödel's results was their impact on Hilbert's program. This impact took the form of a head-on collision in Gödel's second impossibility theorem which very nearly amounts to an announcement of the impossibility of the kind of consistency proof Hilbert was looking for. Hilbert was hoping to prove the consistency of arithmetic by finitistic means, whatever they might be, but in any case by means that do not go beyond elementary arithmetic itself. Accordingly, Gödel's second incompleteness theorem has fairly generally been taken to mean the end of Hilbert's program. Whether this means that Hilbert's entire enterprise was pointless or whether there are other purposes that his metamathematics can serve has been discussed extensively. In order to understand Gödel's work, we do not have to enter this discussion, however.

It is not obvious either that there cannot be methods of proof that go beyond first-order logic and enable us to prove the consistency of arithmetic but which can be argued to be constructive, finitistic or otherwise compatible with Hilbert's requirements. Hilbert's own first reaction was to rely on certain mildly infinitistic methods. Later, Gerhard Gentzen actually proved the consistency of arithmetic by using transfinite induction up to the first undefinable ordinal. Alternatively, one might try to change our basic first-order logic in such a way that consistency proofs become possible. Indeed, Gödel himself experimented with such an interpretation, as will be seen below.

Even though the impact of Gödelian incompleteness on Hilbert's program has received a lion's share of attention in the literature, both historically and systematically its most important repercussions concern other matters. What the incompleteness of formalized first-order arithmetic shows is the need of distinguishing sharply between the truth of arithmetical statements and their provability. What is more, it showed the self-sufficiency and indispensability of model-theoretical concepts and principles. Gödel's result ought to have been taken a virtual declaration of independence of model theory, in that it showed that the model-theoretical notion of arithmetical truth is not exhausted by the proof-theoretical notion of formal provability. Gödel himself emphasized the distinction between truth and provability. However, he did not follow up the suggestions of this contrast, which can be viewed as an example of the general distinction between model theory and proof theory. The reasons for Gödel's failure will be diagnosed later in Chapter 7. The role of his results in the subsequent discussion and even the deeper understanding of these results nevertheless requires an analysis of their impact on the development (and non-development) of the model-theoretical viewpoint in logical theory. This analysis has to be targeted even on the key concept of completeness figuring in Gödel's first incompleteness theorem.

The kind of completeness Gödel's first incompleteness theorem deals with might be called *deductive incompleteness*. It is an attribute of a nonlogical axiom system, such as elementary arithmetic, and it is relative to some given formal method of proving consequences (theorems) from this axiom system. The theory is complete if the consequences include S or ~S for each proposition S that can be

39

formulated in the language of the axiom system. Thus Gödel's first incompleteness theorem shows that any axiomatization of elementary arithmetic are incomplete because there exist a sentence G such that neither G nor ~G is provable on the basis of the axioms.

If the intended theory has only one model, completeness in this sense means that all the sentences true in that one model are formally provable.

But when Gödel proved the semantical completeness of first-order logic, something entirely different was going on. For one thing, the target theory was not a nonlogical axiom system, but a formal system logic. The kind of completeness involved has to be distinguished from deductive completeness. I have called it (following earlier usage) *semantical* completeness. As was explained above, it means that each sentence of a logical language which is true in every model is formally provable. In an equivalent form (assuming the classical negation) it says that whenever a sentence is consistent (in the sense that ~S is not provable), it is true in some model or other.

Gödel never seems to have distinguished this kind of completeness form deductive completeness. The reasons for this *lacuna* will be discussed in Chapter 7 below.

But when it was said earlier that one can formulate by means of second-order logic a *complete* axiom system for elementary arithmetic, neither deductive completeness or semantical completeness was means. (This was in fact that source of the original puzzlement.) What was meant was an attribute of a nonlogical axiom system.

The distinction between the different kinds of completeness is vital for understanding the nature and implications of Gödel's incompleteness theorems. For one thing, it is often said that Gödel has shown the limitations of logic. But what limitations? A limitation must show up in the form of incompleteness of some sort or other. Hence we must ask: What kind of incompleteness did Gödel really prove? The answer to this question is clear. He showed the deductive incompleteness of (first-order) arithmetic. Such incompleteness is relative to a given formal method of logical proof, and it says that no such method can enumerate step by step all (and only) the true sentences of elementary arithmetic. Roughly speaking, there cannot be a computer that I can program in such way that when you push the button, the machine starts listing one by one all the true sentences of elementary arithmetic without your having to interfere in its operation in any way. As was explained, the "computers" meant here are to be understood as the idealized computing architectures called Turing machines.

40

But if this is the only kind of incompleteness involved, we are not dealing with limitations of logic but with limitations of Turing machines. So the question becomes: Does the deductive incompleteness of a nonlogical theory imply any other kinds of incompleteness? The chief candidate is obviously descriptive incompleteness. Is it implied by deductive incompleteness? The intriguing answer to this crucial question is: it depends. It depends on whether the logic that is being used is semantically complete or not. For if a theory T of arithmetic is descriptively complete, it must be categorical, that is, it must have only one model. But if so, all true statements of arithmetic must be consequences of T. If the underlying logic is complete, they must be formally derivable from T, in other words, T must be deductively complete. Since this is excluded by Gödel's first incompleteness theorem, an axiomatic theory of arithmetic cannot be descriptively complete if it uses a semantically complete logic.

Here we can see how the different facets of Gödel's work are interrelated in an intricate, not to say ironic way. Since Gödel was using a logic, namely ordinary first-order logic, which he had himself shown to be semantically complete, he did not see much reason to distinguish deductive completeness and descriptive completeness from each other. This is ironic, in that the distinction between the two is one of the most important instances of the distinction between proof-theoretical and model-theoretical concepts which it was the great merit of Gödel's incompleteness theorems to force upon us.

But are there realistic alternatives to ordinary first-order logic that could be used to reach descriptive completeness in areas like elementary arithmetic? If so these logics must be semantically incomplete. Would not this incompleteness disqualify their claims of being genuine logics?

These questions should prompt a *déjà vu* experience in a perceptive reader. For we have already encountered a logic that seems to fit the bill. It is of course higher-order logic (with the standard interpretation). We have already seen that second-order logic with standard interpretation is semantically incomplete, and we have seen that it can be used to formulate a descriptively complete axiomatization of elementary arithmetic. If higher-order logic with standard interpretation is acknowledged as genuine logic, Gödel's incompleteness theorems do not show that logic has any intrinsic limitations when it comes to descriptive completeness. The importance of this fact is seen especially clearly when we think of what it means to understand a proposition S. Does it mean knowing what all the different models are like in which S is true, that is to say, what conditions the truth S imposes on the world, or does it mean being able to compute purely formally all the consequences of S? I expect most unprejudiced thinkers to agree with me in giving the former answer.

But how can a semantically incomplete logic be a genuine logic? I can counter this with the question: Why should we expect a genuine logic to be semantically complete? Such a logic can be entirely self-sufficient. All the basic notions of such a logic can be defined and used without any reference to proof methods. All the consequence relations of such a logic can depend only on the logical form of the premises and the conclusion. The incompleteness means only that the valid patterns of inference cannot be exhaustively enumerated by a Turing machine. But this is a limitation of Turing machines, not of logic.

Gödel would have agreed. According to him, incompleteness meant that "the kind of reasoning necessary in mathematics cannot be completely mechanized" (quoted by Dawson, 1997, p.263).

But what is meant by completeness? What can be meant by completeness here? If you think about it—and even if you do not think about it—there is more than one way of looking at the idea of completeness. The easier one is seen when the question of completeness is raised in connection with a nonlogical theory like elementary geometry or elementary arithmetic axiomatized above. In such cases, we have a pretty good idea of what it means for an arithmetical statement to be true. For instance, a universally quantified statement $(\forall x) S[x]$ is true of elementary arithmetic and only if $S[n]$ is true for every numeral n. (See Tarski 1956, pp.265-267) The fact that such a truth-definition cannot be expressed in the same first-order language should not bother you, in view of the clear ideas we have of truth—in this case arithmetical truth.

Once we have a truth-definition in place for our formalized arithmetic, for instance for the Robinson arithmetic, we can understand one kind of completeness. Let A be the conjunction of the axioms of Robinson's arithmetic, and let T be an arithmetical truth. Then A is complete if and only if T follows logically from A for each true T.

But what does it mean that T logically follows from A? Here we come to one of the major watersheds of twentieth-century logic. There are two answers to this question. We seem too have a pretty good idea of what it means for A to imply logically T or, in other equivalent words, for T to follow logically from A. It means that there are no conceivable circumstances in which A is true but T is not. An equivalent formulation is to say that the conditional $(A \supset T)$ is logically true, that is, true in all conceivable circumstances. Instead of "all conceivable circumstances" a contemporary logician would say "all models of the language". This notion of completeness is what was referred to earlier as descriptive completeness.

But such definitions of truth (plain truth), logical consequence and logical truth does not say anything about how the applicability of such notions to a particular case can actually be demonstrated. For this purpose, we need formal rules for moving from one formula to another. But since satisfactory mathematical theories are descriptively complete, these formal rules cannot be semantically complete. And, as was seen above, in that case the consistency of the theories in question cannot be demonstrated proof theoretically, as Hilbert hoped to do.

Now what all this implies is that Hilbert's project failed in the last analysis for a reason different from Gödel's second incompleteness theorem. It failed because the logic that is needed in mathematical theories cannot be assumed to be semantically complete.

Gödel's original incompleteness result pertained, not to first-order theories, but to the logical system of Russell's and Whitehead's *Principia Mathematica* ("and related systems"). In other words, it dealt with higher-order logic. Why did he not see that?

The overall picture of the nature of their interplay that has emerged from the post-Gödelian discussion can be characterized in a brief and somewhat oversimplified form as follows: Logic is essentially ordinary first-order logic; this is its core area. This basic logic is semantically complete. It is like the Aristotelian logic in the eyes of Kant: it is essentially complete in the informal sense that no discoveries can be made in it. It is the organon of all reasoning, at least via the mediation of axiomatic first-order set theory, which is the *lingua franca* of mathematics. In general, mathematical theories are (deductively) incomplete, but it is the task of mathematicians to reduce that incompleteness by discovering new axioms. The real progress in the foundations of mathematics thus consists in finding new axioms for set theory. This is the creative component of the foundational studies.

In contrast, a logician's role in mathematics is entirely noncreative. His or her job description is that of a consultant in matters of fallacy avoidance. It is little more than the maintenance of argumentative hygiene in mathematics.

Gödel would not have entirely agreed with this picture. For one thing, he was too well aware of the creative potentialities of logic to assign to it an entirely subordinate role. But he certainly interpreted the creative element in the foundations of mathematics as being essentially the discovery of new axioms. By and large, in a historical perspective this is the overall picture of the respective roles of logic and mathematics that Gödel bequeathed to posterity.

But by this time we have seen enough to realize that some of Gödel's own work suggests an alternative picture. We have seen that ordinary first-order logic is not able to do the job which that logic was originally drafted to do by Frege and by Russell and Whitehead. So why not go beyond this inadequate method and use some more powerful logic instead, for instance second-order logic? Then we presumably have to abandon the semantical completeness of our logic. Gödel's completeness theorem for ordinary first-order logic cannot be extended to these more powerful logics. But even if that is considered a loss, we can gain much more. By giving up the semantical completeness of our logic we remove an obstacle to the formulation of descriptively complete mathematical theories. In a different context, Russell once jokingly described a mathematician as a man who never knows what he is talking about. As long as we cannot formulate descriptively complete theories in mathematics, Russell's joke has a bite. By using semantically incomplete logic, we can hope to reach a point where we do know what we are talking about in mathematics, in the sense of being able to formulate descriptively complete theories for different mathematical theories.

Moreover, what would happen if we be able to so? Then, the creative contribution would no longer be made by the mathematical component. A descriptively complete mathematical theory does not force us to search for new axioms, for the old ones already imply everything. What is needed are stronger and stronger formal rules of logical inference, calculated to capture more and more of the model-theoretical consequence relations. Of course the formulation of the axioms themselves can be a major creative achievement, but it is typically an exercise in conceptual analysis, not in theorem-proving. As far as dealing with the exploration of some field of knowledge by deriving theorems from axioms, the true novelties are better logical proof methods, not new axioms. In a sense, this would vindicate the idea of mathematics as being concerned primarily with proving theorems from axioms. But in this perspective, the axiom systems would be descriptively complete but not deductively complete. Hence the proofs would not rely exclusively on a closed list of rules of inference but might involve the discovery of new valid rules of inference.

Gödel did not himself accept this perspective in so many words. But when we realize that for him set theory was part and parcel of the same study of the Platonic realms of logical entities as first-order logic, his position can be thought of as being analogous to the alternative I have described. In other words, here is an analogy between his vision of the foundations of logic and mathematics and the perspective just adumbrated. What distinguishes his position is his possibly misplaced loyalty to received first-order logic as our true basic logic and to axiomatic set theory as the true higher-order logic.

VII

GÖDEL'S
PHILOSOPHICAL VIEWS

What has been found so far leaves several important questions pending. Why did Gödel not explore the possibilities adumbrated in the preceding chapter? Since he recognized the limitations of proof-theoretical methods, why did he not develop a systematic alternative to them, perhaps in the form of a full-fledged model theory? An answer lies in Gödel's overall philosophy of mathematics—and in his overall philosophical position.

Gödel's failure or reluctance to develop his own major insights systematically has been noted before. For instance, Solomon Feferman, writes that

> it seemed to me that he could well have been more centrally involved in the development of the fundamental concepts of modern logic—truth and compatibility—than he was....
> ...[T]hroughout the 1930's he shied away *from new concepts*

as an object of study as opposed to new concepts as a tool for obtaining results.... [emphasis in the original]

This failure is puzzling in the light of Gödel's creativity and originality. In general, Gödel was conventional and highly inventive in his thinking. Dawson (1997, p. 262) notes "his willingness to countenance possibilities that others were wont to dismiss or overlook" which "served him very well" in his mathematical endeavors. Why, then, his reluctance to develop a systematic model theory, among the other possibilities that his own insights opened? It is fairly obvious that the answer to such questions lies in Gödel's general philosophical assumptions.

How do you classify philosophical positions anyway? Obviously there can be many different classifications but one of the most important contrast that has been operational in contemporary philosophy (and in the history of philosophy) separates what might be called one-world philosophers from many-worlds thinkers. The former are also known as the actualists. They believe that all our meaningful concepts can in the last analysis be analyzed so as to pertaining to our one and only actual world. What else could there be that we would be interested in talking and thinking about? In contrast, other thinkers believe that even when our aim is to deal with the actual world, we can—and sometimes must—use for this purpose concepts whose meaning involves alternatives to the actual state of affairs or courses of events. An example is offered by realistically interpreted probability concepts. If I say that the probability of obtaining two sixes on my next toss of dice is 1/36, I am tacitly considering a number of different possible outcomes of a toss, only one of which will be realized in the actual world. If could not consider other possible outcomes, I would not be able to operate with realistically interpreted probability concepts. Yet these concepts play concrete, important role in actual life. Consider for instance, how you would react if you were told that the probability of obtaining two sixes with the dice you actually playing with is smaller than 1/36.

In philosophy, many-worlds thinking is represented among others by Leibniz according to whose metaphysics a large number of different worlds are metaphysically possible, each of which is governed by its characteristic laws. Out of them, God has chosen one to be actualized. Leibniz was Gödel's favorite philosophers. But one central idea of Leibniz's was never taken up by Gödel: the idea of possible worlds. This is one of the many indications of Gödel's actualism. He agreed for instance in so many words with Russell's statement that logic deals with the real world quite as much as zoology, albeit with its more abstract features. (Cf. above, Chapter 6)

A good test case for the distinction between actualists and many-world thinkers is the notion of logical truth. For a many-world theorist it is essentially the one explained above in Chapter 2: truth on any interpretation, which in a Leibnizian terminology means truth in all possible worlds. In contrast, for an actualist like Gödel logic must be about some aspect of the world.

> Classes and concepts may, however, also be conceived as real objects, namely classes as "pluralities of things" or as structures consisting of a plurality of things and concepts as the properties and relations of things existing independently of our definitions and constructions. (Gödel 1944, p. 137)

But the entities that logic, set theory, and mathematics deal with do not exist in the perceptible part of the world. Hence they must be a nonsensible region of our universe containing the objets of logic and mathematics. The postulation of such a subdomain of abstract entities is what is often referred to as Gödel's "Platonism". This label is a dangerous one, however. Other, unrealized possibilities ("possible worlds") of many-world theorists are in some sense also abstract entities that cannot be perceived by our five senses. However, their conceptual status is radically different from imperceptible denizens of a Platonic region of the actual world. For instance, we cannot perceive how things are in another possible world, not because those "things" are by their own nature imperceptible, but because they belong to a scenario that is by definition unrealized.

One has to be careful not to be misled by terminology here. For instance, the term "world" is not a monopoly of many-world theorists, for the Platonic part of the actual world might be referred to as another "world". Indeed, in his metaphysical and religious speculations Gödel apparently postulated a second "world" which is essentially a realization of all the potentialities existing in this actual universe of ours. (See Dawson 1997, pp. 210-211.)

As far as logical and set-theoretical truths are concerned, for Gödel they are truths about the abstract region of the actual "world". What this means is that there is no sharp distinction between logical and factual truths for Gödel. Both are in a sense factual. Hence for him there is no ultimate difference between deductive and semantical completeness. That ordinary first-order logic is complete while elementary arithmetic is not, is according to this way of thinking merely due to the greater complexity of arithmetic as compared with logic. This is in keeping with the post-Gödelian orthodoxy described in the preceding chapter. It also explains why Gödel never highlighted the fundamental difference between semantical and deductive completeness.

More generally speaking, we can now see why Gödel did not develop one of "the fundamental concepts of modern logic," the concept of truth, to quote Feferman again. Since truth is the most important concept of model theory, we can now answer why the question as to why Gödel did not develop a systematic model theory, even though his own results seem to have motivated it. The answer is that Gödel's philosophical beliefs implied that model theory was, if not impossible, then largely irrelevant to philosophically and for the purposes of deeper theoretical understanding of the foundations of mathematics. The reason is that to do model theory is to consider a variety of different interpretations of the nonlogical concepts one is dealing with. But according to Gödel there is in effect only one relevant interpretation of mathematical language, viz. the one in which mathematical terms refer to the citizens of the Platonic realm of objects within our actual world. Small wonder, therefore, that Gödel did not develop a systematic model theory or a general theory of truth, leaving the latter task to Tarski. Gödel was fully aware of the need of model-theoretical notions, especially of the notion of truth, in the foundations of mathematics. However, as Feferman notes, he used them as tools for obtaining results within an established framework rather than as objects of study.

Philosophically, Gödel used the indispensability of concepts like the notion of truth to emphasize the objective character of mathematical objects and of logical and mathematical truths. He also used it to criticize the view of philosophy as the study of the logical syntax of language. He was aware of specific results concerning the notion of truth, for instance of the undefinability of arithmetical truth in first-order arithmetical language. But Gödel never developed these insights systematically in the way Tarski did only a couple of years later. In a wide historical perspective, Gödel's incompleteness theorem was the first and foremost result that forced logicians, mathematicians and philosophers to realize the need of distinguishing between provability and truth. But Gödel's philosophical views, which he apparently developed at an early stage of his career, prevented him from breaking the mold of one-world thinking and developing a genuine model

49

theory. One of the remarkable things about Gödel's one-world conviction is that it unmistakably reflects his personality, as we found it in Chapter 2 above. We found there a curious combination of insecurity and critical intelligence in Gödel. He needed an accepted framework within which he could safely operate, and was extremely reluctant to venture beyond it. Within such a framework, he could be critical, conjuring up with his marvelous acuity and invention all sorts of surprising and sometimes disconcerting results. However, these results were not supposed to upset the safe framework or venture beyond it. Gödel's actualism is but a case in point. Gödel does not dare to leave the familiar ground of the actual world and venture to speculate about unrealized possibilities. The idea that logically and philosophically crucial concepts, such as meaning and logical truth, can (and must) be defined in terms of a range of different scenarios (aka possible worlds) is completely foreign to him. This is the motivation of Gödel's Platonism. He has to construe the meaning of all the crucial concepts by reference to the actual world which in effect means finding a slot for logical and mathematical objects in the actual world and construe logical and mathematical truths as being about this world of ours. This is also the reason why Gödel did not develop any systematic model theory.

The attribution of this motivation to Gödel might seem speculative. However, it is only one example of many of Gödel's preference of a generally accepted framework even when there are good reasons to doubt its adequacy. Later we will briefly examine two frameworks which Gödel accepted and stuck to even though doubts can be raised about their ultimate adequacy. The two most important examples are the received first-order logic and first-order axiomatic set theory.

Gödel's actualism led him also to epistemological problems and not only to metaphysical ones. For how are we supposed to come to know the abstract Platonic region of our world? Not by sense-perception, for we are by definition dealing with abstract, imperceptible entities. Hence Gödel has to assume a nonsensible access to his Platonic realm. This method of access is his famous (or notorious) notion of intuition. Intuition is for Gödel a logician's counterpart to sense-perception. Its nature and status nevertheless involve serious philosophical problems. In light of what has been found, it can be seen that this problem is self-inflicted or, rather, inflicted on us by Gödel's one-world assumption. If we do not make it, we do not need the postulation of such an "extra-sensory perception"—for that is what

50

Gödel's intuition ultimately is. Kripke has tried to ridicule possible-worlds theorists by asking what kind of telescope it is by means of which they can establish what there is in other possible worlds. This is a bad joke, for unrealized possible scenarios by definition do not exist to be observed by a telescope any more than by a naked intuition. They are precisely the possibilities that were not, or will not be, realized. The real butt of Kripke's joke is not a possible-world theorist but a philosopher who believes in an actually existing supersensory region of the real world. It is not Montague or David Lewis who is the correct target of Kripke's pointed question, but Gödel.

Gödel's own comparison between mathematicians on the one hand and physical scientists on the other shows the weaknesses of his notion of intuition as a source of logical and mathematical truths. Gödel describes his position as follows (1944, p. 137):

> Classes and concepts, however, also be conceived as real objects namely classes a "pluralities of things" or as structures consisting of a plurality of things and concepts as properties and relations of things existing independently of our definitions and constructions.
>
> It seems to me that the assumption of such objects is quite legitimate as the assumption of physical bodies and there is therefore quite as much reason to believe in their existence.

But scientists do not just postulate physical objects. They manipulate physical objects, construct them and experiment with them. The question of the existence of physical objects does not arise in science or even in the philosophy of science. A physicist does not merely observe phenomena and hen try to devise a generalization to capture them. A physicist can take an active role in the course of events. He or she can create the kinds of systems (as a physicist would call them) that will have to be among the models (in logicians' sense of the term) of a sought-for theory or of an already known theory—if it is to be true. Likewise, a many-world logician (alias model theorist) can construct isomorphic replicas of unrealized possibilities as parts of the actual world, either as parts of its more concrete or its more abstract regions. But this presupposes a variety of possible models for the language of the theory not just one fixed structure in the Platonic part of the actual universe. Thus Gödel's one-world outlook forces him to defend his idea of intuition by means of an oversimplified, static conception of methodology of physical sciences. His notion of mathematical intuition is a product of this oversimplified conception. Mathematical intuition is supposed to be an analogue to perception, but counterparts to scientific experimentation and generalization in logic and mathematics. It follows from the job description of Gödelian intuition as giving us access to the abstract Platonic region that it cannot be restricted to direct cognitive relation to particular objects. This distinguishes Gödel's concept of intuition, as he notes himself (Wang, 1997 pp. 217-218), from both Kant's and Hilbert's notion of intuition. Likewise, Gödel differs sharply from Kant as to the reasons why intuitions can give us *a priori* knowledge. Kantian intuitions can yield such knowledge because their introduction merely reproduces the operations through which we impose the forms of space and time on objects and through which we have individuated those objects. We can in other words intuitively anticipate the applicability of those forms to experience because we have ourselves projected them to objects. For this reason a Kantian intuition can yield knowledge even "without any object being present, either previously or now, to which it could refer" (Kant *Prolegomena*, sec. 8). According to Kant, the use of *a priori* intuitions is not like perceiving an object. It is like introducing a representation of some particular unknown object in anticipation of any perceptual knowledge thereof. This is all in sharp contrast to Gödel for whom intuition could access mind-independent reality. The very point of those aspects of objects of which Kantian intuitions could enlighten us was that they were for Kant mind-dependent.

One is tempted to suggest that Gödel's own practice belied his own theory of mathematical knowledge as based on mathematical intuition. What I have in mind is his work in axiomatic set theory. According to his official view, what we are doing there is to try to capture the set of sentences true in the universe of set theory as logical consequences of the axioms of set theory. Of course any actual axiomatization of set theory is incomplete. Hence what we must try to do according to Gödel is to hone our intuitions and hope that they yield new, stronger axioms. Gödel made some interesting suggestions as to what such novel axioms might be like. These suggestions are not made on the basis of naked intuition, however, but by reference to the model-theoretical properties of the set-theoretical universe. Among other ideas he surmised that suitable maximality assumptions not unlike Hilbert's axiom of completeness in geometry (see Gödel 1986-, vol. 2, pp. 167 – 168) might be what is needed in the foundations of set theory. It seems to me that Gödel's intuitions can be sharpened further here and that the real challenge in set theory is to find an equilibrium of maximality and minimality assumptions: the set of natural numbers must be minimal at the same time as there must be as many sets as possible. (Cf. Hintikka 1993.)

Be these intuitions as they may, Gödel was not content in his own work to stare at the axioms of set theory and at their known consequences and wait for his intuition to tell him what further axioms are available in the away one is tempted to imagine Quine as having done when he proposed his stratified axiom system for set theory. In his consistency proof for the continuum Gödel's actualism had some surprising consequences. As was mentioned in Chapter 2, he believed in a version of Anselm's ontological proof of God's existence. At first sight, a connection with this belief and Gödel's actualism is not obvious. It is nevertheless there. Anselm argued that we must be able to think of the most perfect being, and since existence is one of the perfections, that perfect being must exist. Now it is not difficult to establish by purely logical means similar conclusions, for instance, that there is an individual such that, if it exists, everything exists. The difficulty comes in with the question as to whether that most perfect being in our world is the same as the most perfect being in some other possible world. Why cannot a model polytheist believe that different divinities are the most perfect beings in their respective worlds? Gödel's actualism led him to disregard these crucial difficulties and thereby to overestimate the force of the ontological argument. Once again, what looks like a weird theological view is little more than a testimony to the courage of Gödel's basic logical and metaphysical assumptions.

A discussion of Gödel's philosophical ideas would not be complete without pointing out how even his most abstruse scientific results were philosophically motivated and had philosophical implications—at least in Gödel's own mind. The most important case in point is his work on the general theory of relativity, inspired by his discussions with Einstein. What Gödel did was to discover a family of solutions to the fundamental equations of Einstein's general theory of relativity. These solutions had the surprising feature that time had in them a circular structure. Gödel thought that these results might support idealistic philosophies which deny the reality of time. Even though Gödel did not point it out, they also seem to have similarities with philosophical theories of "eternal return."

VIII

GÖDEL AS A SET
THEORIST

Gödel believed that there is a Platonic region of abstract entities as a part of our actual world. What is that region like according to Gödel? How can we find out?

For Gödel, at least part of an answer was obvious. The abstract entities we need in mathematics are primarily sets or entities that can be defined in terms of sets, such as functions. Hence an important part of the exploration of the Platonic world was for him set theory. Thus it is not surprising that Gödel should have devoted much of his time to work to problems of set theory. According to Hao Wang's impressions, Gödel "spent more time (perhaps from 1931 to 1946) thinking about set theory than about other areas of mathematical logic."

Likewise, it is not surprising that Gödel's attention should have directed among other things to two crucial questions that have already been mentioned, namely, to the continuum problem and to the status of the axiom of choice. The former problem is obviously one of the most fundamental ones in the entire set theory, hence one of the most fundamental ones in Gödel's ontology of abstract entities. The status

54

of the continuum problem had been canonized by David Hilbert when he listed it as one of the most important unsolved problems in mathematics in his famous address to the 1900 Paris Congress of mathematics.

If one believes in first-order axiomatization as the right approach to set theory, as most people seem to do nowadays, one must ascribe to Gödel one of the most remarkable results concerning the continuum hypothesis. He did not manage to prove the truth of the generalized continuum hypothesis, but he was able to do the next best thing, namely to prove its possibility in the sense of its formal compatibility with the axioms of set theory. If this axiom system has any models, then in some of them the generalized continuum hypothesis is also true. In other words the usual axioms of first-order set theory do not logically imply a negative answer to the continuum problem.

In June 1937, Gödel found an argument to this effect. He also found a proof of the consistency of the axiom of choice with the other usual set-theoretical axioms.

This is an impressive intellectual achievement. Gödel's results were complemented in 1963 by the results of Paul Cohen. Cohen proved the inverse of Gödel's results. Not only is the negation of the continuum hypothesis not provable from the axioms of set theory. The hypothesis itself is not provable, according to Paul Cohen, from the same axioms. In other words, the continuum hypothesis is independent of the usual axiomatic set theory. If we want to solve the continuum problem in terms of an axiomatic set theory, we have somehow to discover (or invent) new axioms, just as Gödel suggested. Likewise, the axiom of choice has been shown to be independent of the usual axioms of set theory.

Gödel's result is not entirely surprising. What is or at least should be surprising is the way he proved it. Gödel was seen not to have wanted to build a systematic model theory. Yet his line of thought in his consistency proof was model-theoretical rather than proof-theoretical. What Gödel did was to define (or in a natural sense of the word, construct) a certain model L for all the axioms of set theory (except for the axiom of choice). Then he shows that the generalized continuum hypothesis and the axiom of choice are also true in L. This is of course sufficient to show that the continuum hypothesis and the axiom of choice are compatible with the (other) usual axioms of set theory.

The intuitive idea in constructing L step by step is a kind of ontological economy. Gödel admits into the model L at any stage only such sets as can be defined by means of quantifiers ranging over the sets so far admitted into the model L. Strictly speaking, this does not represent the stingiest possible parsimony, but comes close to it. In 1963 Paul Cohen modified Gödel's construction so as to obtain a model that is in a specifiable sense a minimal one. Thus it is the other axioms of set theory (besides the axiom of choice) that determine what is included in L. They include the following requirements:

(S.1)   There is an empty set.

(S.2)   For any set α, there is a set $\{\alpha\}$ with α as its only member.

(S.3)   For any two sets α, β, there is a set $\{\alpha, \beta\}$ whose members are α and β.

(S.4)   For any set α there is a set $P(\alpha)$ whose members are all the subsets of α. This $P(\alpha)$ is called the power set of α.

(S.5)   The sum of all members of any set is a set.

Over and above (S.1) – (S.4), the usual assumptions of set theory include the following:

(S.5)   Sets with the same members are identical (extensionality)

(S.6)   The sets y bearing a definable relation A(y,x) to the members of a given set α form a set. In the notation of logic books, for any formula with two variables A(y,x) and for any set α,
$\{y: (\exists x)(x \in \alpha \ \& \ A(x,y))\}$ is also a set.

(S.7)   There is a set β that contains the empty set and contains $\{\alpha\}$ for any $\alpha \in \beta$.

This last axiom guarantees that the models of set theory are infinite.

This axiomatization is known as the Zermelo-Fraenkel (ZF) set theory. There are other, essentially equivalent axiomatizations, including what is known as von Neumann-Bernays set theory.

What Gödel does is to construct a hierarchy of sets K_β indexed by what set-theorist call ordinal numbers β. He takes as his starting point

K_0 the empty set. The rest of the hierarchy is defined by two requirements

(1) $K_{\beta+1} = D(K_\beta)$
(2) $K_\gamma = U_{\beta<\gamma} K_\beta$

where $D(K_\beta)$ is all the definable subsets of K_β and UK_β is the set-theoretical sum of all sets K_β (subject to restrictions on β). The ordinal numbers needed here are definable set-theoretical entities. The totality L of sets obtainable in this way is well defined set-theoretically. It is known as Gödel's constructible universe. It is not difficult to see that all the axioms of set theory are true when relativized to L. That is, that L is a model of the Zermelo-Fraenkel set theory. Gödel was able to show also that the axiom of choice and the generalized continuum hypothesis are both true in L. This shows the consistency of the generalized continuum hypothesis and the axiom of choice relative to the ZF set theory.

Since L is definable in set theory, we can formulate in axiomatic set theory the claim that it is an entire model of set theory. This can be written as L = V, and it is known as the axiom of constructibility.

Is this axiom itself true? Intuitively, the answer is fairly obviously negative. The whole idea underlying set theory is for it to be a theory of all possible sets. If so, the axiom of constructibility, which severely restricts the citizenship in the land of set theory, cannot very well characterize the intended model of set theory. Indeed, Gödel himself apparently believed that the intended set-theoretical universe is best characterized by means of suitable maximality assumptions, perhaps comparable with Hilbert's so-called axiom of completeness in the foundations of geometry.

The constructible hierarchy is nevertheless very interesting. It has interesting connections on the one hand with the minimal models of axiomatic set theory and on the other hand with what is in our days generally taken to be the standard model of set theory, known as the cumulative hierarchy of sets. It is obtained from Gödel's construction by replacing in (1) $D(K_\beta)$ by $P(K_\beta)$, in other words by the power set of K_β. Thus Gödel's work on the constructible hierarchy has strongly influenced later mathematicians' and philosophers' ideas about set theory.

From the vantage point of his own incompleteness results (and of Tarski's related results) Gödel's work on first-order axiomatic set theory nevertheless cannot but strike one as perplexing, not to say paradoxical. Not only had Gödel shown that the notions of truth and provability have to be distinguished sharply in arithmetic. He had shown that arithmetical truths cannot be exhausted by any axiomatization. Since elementary arithmetic can be reconstructed in set theory, the same limitations apply to axiomatizations of set theory. Why, then, did he choose to approach set theory in terms of first-order axiomatizations?

Gödel's answer might have been to allege that this is best we can do. Deductive incompleteness is a fact of logician's life. There is no point in trying to get around it. The best we can do is to experiment with various stronger axioms of set theory suggested to us by our mathematical intuition, fully aware that whatever true new axioms we might find will leave set theory still incomplete and set others to still looking for further axioms.

Perhaps mathematicians are condemned by logic to such a Sisyphean toil. However, it is hard not to suspect that Gödel's insecurity was again in operation in his choice of an approach to set theory. The descriptive incompleteness of axiomatic set theory is due to its being a first-order theory. Now a first-order axiomatic set theory was precisely the kind of safe, accepted framework that he longed for. Within it, he could even practice model theory, even though he never constructed a general model theory. For the consistency proof for the generalized continuum hypothesis outlined above is more naturally thought of as a model-theoretical rather than a proof theoretical one.

But further doubts are possible here. Set theory is often considered as an appropriate framework for doing model theory, perhaps even doing the entire job of model theory. If so, the question arises whether it can serve as a framework of its own model theory. Indeed, Gödel's construction of L was carried out within axiomatic set theory. But what happens to the most central ingredient of model theory, to truth-definitions, in axiomatic set theory? Obviously one can formulate what looks like the right truth conditions in set theory. For instance consider a sentence of the form:

(3) $(\forall x)(\exists y)\ S[x,y]$

When is it true? Obviously if an only if one can find, for each individual x, an individual y (depending, of course, on x) such that $S[x,y]$. This y is a "witness individual" which guarantees that $(\exists y)\ S[x,y]$ is true for the given x. This clearly means that there is a function f such that

(4) $(\forall x)\, S[x,f(x)]$

Such "witness functions" have a technical name in logic. They are known as Skolem functions. Hence (3) is true if and only if a Skolem function exists for it. Now the existence of such a Skolem function can be expressed set-theoretically. The set theoretical statement asserting such existence would be the translation of the second-order sentence

(5) $(\exists f)(\forall x)\, S[x,f(x)]$

into the language of set theory. The same things can be said of each sentence of a first-order language. Each of them has a truth condition that asserts the existence of a number of functions that govern the choice of the "witness individuals that verify the sentence. These functions are its Skolem functions. These truth conditions are quite as natural as in the special case. Moreover, they can all be combined in a single presumptive truth definition, which seems to implement very well our pretheoretical ("intuitive") ideas about truth.

But according to Tarski's impossibility theorem, mentioned in Chapter 5 above, no first-order theory allows the formulation of a truth definition for itself. Hence at least one of the truth conditions must be false. Such a condition takes the form of a sentence which is true but which does not have functions that provide its witness individuals. In principle, the situation is as if (3) were true in a model of set theory even though (4) is false for every function f. But the existence of such a function is what the truth of (3) means according to our common sense—or is it common intuition?

What does this conundrum amount to? There is not inconsistency present. The day can be saved technically by adopting a nonstandard interpretation of second-order quantifier. I suspect that Gödel was prepared to do so. But a serious theoretical problem still remains. When we are taking the existence of a function f in (4) as a truth condition of (3), we are naturally adopting a standard reading of the existential quantifier $(\exists f)$. But if so, there are models of axiomatic set theory in which some sentences are false that are intuitively speaking true.

Now appeals to our "pretheoretical ideas" or to people's "intuitions" always have to be taken with a grain of salt. Perhaps the clash between what is said to be true in the models of axiomatic set theory and some people's "intuitions" is not very serious, it might be suggested. However, the intuitions that I am appealing to are the intuitions on which the very meaning of the standard interpretation of quantification over sets and functions is based. And the meaning of the continuum hypothesis is in turn predicated on the standard interpretation. This hypothesis says that there is a set which can be mapped one-one into a set of the cardinality $2^{\aleph_0}$ but which cannot be mapped one-one or a set of the cardinality $\aleph_0$. This "can be mapped" means obviously the existence of any arbitrary function doing the mapping, that is, any function in the standard sense. If the standard intuitions are violated by an axiomatic set theory, then the provability of any statement from the axioms of that set theory does not automatically show anything about its truth or falsity. In such a situation, formal consistency results of the kind Gödel and Paul Cohen proved have no direct implications concerning the truth of the continuum hypothesis. In arithmetic, Gödel was the first major figure to emphasize the difference between truth and provability. In first-order axiomatic set theory, we find an even more radical difference between what is true and what is provable.

Thus Gödel's caution led him to remain within the framework of first-order axiomatic set theory which not only restricted his theoretical horizon in this direction but also leads us to wonder, in the light of hindsight, how significant his work in set theory is in the last analysis.

The same line of thought has implications also for the axiom of choice. Indeed, the implication from (3) to (5) can be considered as a form of the axiom of choice. What was said of the role of Skolem functions as providing us with the "witness individuals" satisfying the truth of the sentence whose Skolem functions they are amounts to a strong intuitive reason for accepting the axiom of choice. The same reason supports any implication from a sentence to the existence of its Skolem functions. But there are the implications that do not all hold in the models of first-order axiomatic set theory. Hence this axiomatic set theory in a sense violates the intuitions on which the axiom of choice is based.

IX

THE DIALECTIC OF GÖDEL'S *DIALECTICA* INTERPRETATION

Gödel would not have been the genius that he was if he had remained perfectly happy with the overall picture of logic and mathematics that many of his contemporaries and successors have adopted. Among his few published writings there is a short paper which is in so many words calculated to venture in a new direction. It has the involved title *"Über eine bisher noch nicht benützte Erweiterung des finiten Standpunktes"* ("On a so far unexploited extension of the finitistic point of view"). It appeared in the Swiss journal *Dialectica* in 1958. It is not clear what motivated Gödel to write it, but it is a self-conscious attempt to explore certain new lines of thought, and it can be taken to foreshadow certain highly interesting subsequent developments. At first sight, what Gödel does might seem puzzling, and the author provides few clues. What Gödel does is technically to present an interpretation of first-order logic and elementary arithmetic. This translation takes initially the form of a translation: each expression of a first-order arithmetic is translated into an expression of the corresponding higher-order language (higher-order theory of arithmetic). After that, all function variables (of any order) occurring in the translations are restricted to recursive values. (This is one of the few occasions on which Gödel puts the notion of recursity to work for a general theoretical purpose.)

The translation rules look relatively simple on paper. Gödel associates with each formula two function variables that can be of any logical type (order), that is, first-order, second-order, third-order etc. Then the translation rules might be expressed as follows:

(A & B) = (A, (ξ, ψ) & B(ζ, φ)) has the translation (A & B)* = ($\exists\xi$)($\exists\zeta$)($\forall\psi$)($\forall\varphi$)(A*(ξ,ψ) & B*(ζ,ψ)) where A* and B* are two translations of A and B, respectively.

(A $\vee$ B) = (A(ξ,ψ) $\vee$ B(ζ, φ)) has the translation (A $\vee$ B)* = ($\exists\xi$)($\exists\zeta$)($\exists\rho$)($\forall\psi$)($\forall\varphi$) ((A*(ξ,ψ) & ρ = 0) $\vee$ (B*(ζ, φ) & $\rho \neq$ 0))

The conditional (A $\supset$ B) = (A(ξ,ψ) $\supset$ B(ζ, φ)) has the translation (A $\supset$ B)* = ($\exists\Psi$)($\exists\Phi$)($\forall\xi$)($\forall\varphi$)((A*(ξ,ψ(ξ,φ)) $\supset$ B*(ϕ(ξ),φ)) Here Ψ and Φ are of a higher type (order) than ψ and φ.

The negation ~A=~A(ξ,ψ) has the translation (~A)* = ($\exists\Phi$)($\forall\xi$) ~ A*(ξ,Φ(ξ))

But what do these translation rules mean? What is their theoretical motivation? It looks as if one could set up hundreds of similar translation recipes. Why these particular ones? When I first saw Gödel's rules, I could not make heads or tails of them. Only much later did I find a way of relating them to wider theoretical issues in the foundations of mathematics, only to discover that Dana Scott had hit on the same idea earlier.

What is this idea? To me it first came with the force of a sudden revelation. Gödel's rules can be understood as rules in certain games of verification and falsification. The two new variables range over the strategies of the two players, the verifier and the falsifier. From this perspective, everything in Gödel's rules suddenly makes sense.

In fact, the same game-theoretical interpretation can be applied to ordinary first-order logic, and is easier to understand there. Mathematicians routinely express existential quantifiers by speaking of what "one can find," and existence is in several natural languages expressed by similar locutions, for instance the Swedish *det finns*. Hilbert had tried to capture this idea by defining quantifiers in terms of certain choice functions codified by what he called epsilon terms. For instance, (εx) A(x) is supposed to stand for an arbitrary individual" satisfying A(x) is supposed to stand for an "arbitrary individual" satisfying A(x). A more systematic way of implementing this way of thinking and speaking is associated with each first-order sentence S a two-person game G(S) relative to a model of the language to which S belongs. There are two players, the verifier and the falsifier. (The latter can be thought of as nature or as a malicious Cartesian demon.) The rules of the game are as follows:

(G.$\lor$) G($S_1 \lor S_2$) begins with the verifier's choice of S_1 or S_2, say S_2. The game is then continued as in G(S_2)

(G.&) G(S & S_2) begins likewise, except that the falsifier makes the choice.

(G.E) G(($\exists$x) S[x]) begins by a choice by the verifier of an individual from the universe of discourse. If the name of the choice individual is b, the game is continued as in G(S[b])

(G.A) G(($\forall$x) S[x]) begins likewise, except that the falsifier makes the choice

(G.~) G(~G) begins with an exchange of roles of the two players, as defined by these rules. After that, the game is continued as in G(S).

After a finite number of moves, the players reach an atomic sentence or an identity A. Such sentences have an interpretation independently of the meaning of logical constants. If A is true, the verifier wins; if it is false, the falsifier wins. The sentence S is true if and only if there exists in G(S) a winning strategy for the initial falsifier. A winning strategy is a strategy that results independently of the strategy that one's opponent chooses. In other words, even if the opponent finds out which strategy you are following, he, she or it cannot use this information to win the play.

These rules of definitions define a semantics for, and an interpretation of, ordinary first-order languages which is equivalent

63

with the usual one. What happens in Gödel's interpretation is that he modifies the rules so as to obtain a nonclassical interpretation of logic and arithmetic. It is not hard to see how he does it. The main change is that Gödel restricts all the strategies (strategy functions) to recursive (computable) ones. This is in keeping with his attempt to keep as close to the finitistic point of view as possible.

Once this is seen the motivation of Gödel's disjunction rule becomes transparent. He is requiring that the verifier has a way (part of his/her/its winning strategy) of computing which disjunct of each disjunction is true.

The rule for conditionals is somewhat complicated. What is involved are several requirements. One of them says that if there is a winning verification strategy ξ in the game played with the antecedent A, that is, which wins against any falsification strategy even if it is allowed to depend on ξ, the knowledge of this ξ enables the verifier to have a winning strategy $\Phi(\xi)$ in the game with the consequent B. Conversely, if there is a falsifying strategy φ in the game with B, knowing it will help to find a falsifying strategy $\Psi(\xi,\varphi)$ in the game with the antecedent.

The negation rule says that the verifier does not have a winning strategy. If the verifier tries a strategy ξ, there exists a falsifier strategy $\Phi(\xi)$ which defeats ξ.

What is remarkable about this negation rule is that it codifies the "classical" contradictory negation. It would have been possible for Gödel to interpret negation dually, that is, to require that A not—A is true if and only if the falsifier has a winning falsificatory strategy in the game with A. This idea can be implemented by the following Gödelian rule:

$$(\exists \xi)(\forall \Phi) \sim A^*(\Phi(\xi),\xi)$$

This actually reduces to $\sim A^*$.

One remarkable thing here is that Gödel keeps the negation classical, that is, that his negation is the contradictory negation $\sim S$ which is true as soon as S is not, even if there does not exist any winning strategy for the falsifier. If he had formulated the negation rule otherwise, he would have had obtained a logic with a "mirror-image" strong negation and avoided any ascent beyond second-order languages. (This would have necessitated a reformulation also of the rule for conditionals.) An especially innovative feature of Gödel's interpretation is that he is chaning the interpretation of om logic, not only by changing the rules governing individual logical notions but restricting the verifier's strategies.

There is no documentary evidence that Gödel himself ever motivated his *Dialectica* interpretation by using game-theoretical terminology and concepts. But it is very hard not to believe that he did not follow a line of thought tantamount to the one sketched above. Game theory was created by Gödel's Königsberg admirer and sometime colleague at the Institute of Advanced Studies, John von Neumann. The game-theoretical interpretation of quantifiers had been put forward (unbeknownst to Gödel) already by Peirce, and later a version of the same interpretation was spontaneously and independently adopted by several logicians when they were confronted by extensions of first-order logic where the usual semantics (interpretation) fails, for instance in the study of branching quantifiers, game quantifiers and infinitely deep logics. Later the game-theoretical semantics for different logics has been systematized, and has opened several interesting new perspectives on the foundations of logic and mathematics.

Thus Gödel's *Dialectica* interpretation anticipates one of the most important subsequent developments in the philosophy of logic and mathematics. Even though these developments are not a part of the story of Kurt Gödel, a brief indication of their impact is in order. One important thing that a game-theoretical interpretation does is to focus (logicians') attention to dependence relations between the different quantifiers in a given sentence. For instance,

$$(\forall x)(\exists y) \ S[x,y]$$

the quantifier $(\exists y)$ depends on the quantifier $(\forall x)$ in the sense that the verifiers winning choice of a value of y depends on the falsifier's choice of a value of y. This dependence is in game-theoretical semantics captured by the idea that the move connected with $(\forall x)$ is in the information set of the move connected with $(\exists y)$. what this means is simply that the player making the latter move is aware of the outcome of the former move. This dependence is also tantamount to a dependence of the variable y on the variable x.

Now it is clear that an adequate logical language must be capable of expressing all possible patterns of dependence and independence between variables, and hence all possible patterns of dependence and independence between quantifiers. Bu when this is realized, it also becomes clear that the "ordinary" received first-order logic is incapable of doing so. If a dependence relation is expressed by the inverse of an arrow, the following patterns cannot be expressed in the received first-order logic:

Thus:

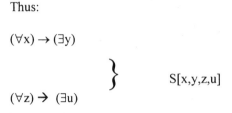

$$(\forall x) \rightarrow (\exists y)$$

$$(\forall z) \rightarrow (\exists u)$$

$$S[x,y,z,u]$$

The ordinary first-order logic can be extended so as to make these expressible, while still remaining on the first-order level. The result has been called independence-friendly (IF) logic, even though this label may not be a completely happy one.

Even though some of the crucial ideas on which this logic is based were anticipated by Gödel, it ws not worked out by him, nor were the perspectives it opens explored by him. It is not even clear whether Gödel had any awareness of these perspectives. In the rest of his work, he was happy to work within the established framework of received first-order logic and its familiar extensions, such as nonstandard higher-order logic and intuitionistic logic. However, the general perspective in which we have to view Gödel's main results and their implications is affected by the new logic. One striking thing about IF first-order logic is that it is semantically incomplete. Hence, if this logic rather than the received first-order logic is the general, unrestricted logic of quantifiers, Gödel's completeness proof loses much of its philosophical significance. It does not any longer show that the received first-order logic is complete. Rather, logicians will be like housewives: their work is never done.

On the other hand, as was seen in Chapter 6, the semantical incompleteness of IF logic makes it possible to try to use it or one of its extensions, to formulate descriptively complete theories where the received first-order logic was incapable of doing so. More generally speaking, the division of labor between logic and mathematics described in Chapter 6, must be reconsidered.

As far as Gödel himself is concerned, we can see the same pattern repeated her as was found in his treatment of completeness and incompleteness. Gödel discovered new, potentially revolutionary ideas, but instead of using them as a basis of new theories he preferred to stay within an already established framework. One can even see his actualism in operation here.   Gödel's *Dialectica* interpretation was presented above as a new way of defining the crucial model-theoretical concept of (plain material) *truth.* Gödel himself nevertheless compares it with Heyting's intuitionistic first-order logic, which of   course is a deductive system for systematizing intuitionistically valid *logical* truth. In the later discussion, it is sometimes dealt with as one, sometimes as the other.   Gödel is apparently dealing   with logical truth as if it were a variant of simpler material truth.

X

TURING MACHINES OR GÖDEL'S MACHINES?

Gödel's achievements are not exhausted by the ones so far discussed. One of the most consequential of them grew out of Gödel's work on completeness and incompleteness. In explaining that work and its consequences, I have repeatedly referred to what is computable and what can be done purely mechanically. These locutions are intended to mean the same, but what is this one and the same thing? This question was made an important one in the thirties by developments like Gödel's incompleteness theorem. It can be formulated as the question: Which functions are effectively (mechanically) computable? (Computability can her be taken to be roughly equivalent with what can be calculated by an idealized computer which has unlimited memory and an unlimited amount of time.) This question was addressed by several logicians including Gödel. In a paper published in 1934 he suggested that computable functions might be identified with general recursive functions, that is, functions definable by a finite number of recursive equations of the kind that can be used to define the basic arithmetical operations.

Examples of such equations are offered by the axioms (A.1) – (A.7) of Robinson arithmetic. (See Chapter 3.) Gödel was not certain himself that his characterization really did its job. Could there be types of recursion not captured by his definition of general recursive function? Moreover, soon other logicians offered other definitions of effectively computable functions. Among them there were the notions defined by Post, Church, Kleene, and Markov. The best known is the characterization of effectively computable functions by Alan Turing in terms of what can be calculated by means of certain simple idealized computers that have come to be known as Turing machines. Their basic idea was explained above. These characterizations are on the surface quite unlike, using different frameworks of ideas. For instance, Church's characterization is in terms of a special logical calculus, known as the lambda calculus. Which of them is the right one? The surprising answer—surprising, that is to say, to Gödel's contemporaries—is: All of the above. In one of the most impressive developments in logic in the twentieth century, all these different characterizations of effective computability turned out to be equivalent. This remarkable convergence also strongly suggests that these definitions really capture the important idea of computability. The claim that they do is known as Church's thesis. Together, the work that went to these definitions was one of the most important starting points of theoretical computer science. The systematic study of computability in the sense of these definitions is known as the theory of recursive functions and effective computability.

Gödel's definition was the first one of this interesting proliferation of characterizations. He thus occupies an interesting position in the history of the theory of computing. But, as Feferman pointed out, Gödel never developed a systematic theory of computability himself. In spite of Gödel's pioneering role, it is therefore perhaps no great historical injustice that effective computability is in out days most commonly referred to as Turing machine computability.

Gödel was nevertheless deeply interested in the philosophical questions concerning computers and computability. The most interesting questions which occupied him and which have since provoked an intensive discussion are prompted by his own incompleteness result. It has been said more than once above that what Gödel's result certainly brings out are limitations of computers (Turing machines), not any intrinsic limitation of logic. Since logic is presumably the medium of human thinking, this suggests that the human mind can do more than any computer, and hence cannot be a computer. This suggestion was adopted by Gödel himself. Later, several authors, including Lucas and Roger Penrose, have argued extensively for the conclusion that Gödel's impossibility theorem shows that human minds cannot be computers—at least not Turing machines.

This entire discussion is confused, however. It may be true in some sense that the human mind operates in a way different from the *modus operandi* of a Turing machine, and even that Gödel's theorem shows this difference. However, the arguments offered in the literature are for the most part highly unsatisfactory. For one thing, what is it that humans are supposed to know but machines not? Presumably the existence of a true but unprovable arithmetical proposition. But Gödel's argument does not prove the existence of absolutely unprovable arithmetical truths. Its conclusion is relative to some given first-order axiom system of elementary arithmetic, such as the Robinson arithmetic explained in Chapter 3 above, and proves only that there is a true proposition unprovable in that particular system. There are plenty of other systems in which that same proposition is mechanically provable.

Secondly, what Gödel proved is not even the existence of a true proposition unprovable in the given system, but only that if that system is consistent, *then* such a paradoxical sentence exists. In order for a human mind or for a computer to know the existence of a Gödelian sentence, he, she, or it must know the consistency. But how is either one supposed to know that?

Even more importantly, the alleged implications of Gödel's impossibility theorem for the relation of human minds to machines rest mostly on a shallow conception of what thinking is either in the case of humans or of people. In effect, the limits of thinking are identified with what one can prove by means of logical rules of inference. But the phrase "by means of" is a tricky one. One's actual thinking is not guided by such rules of inference, no matter whether one is a human being or a Turing machine. The simple reason is that the so-called rules of inference are merely permissive. They do not tell us what to do; they merely tell us what we *may* do while avoiding logical fallacies. Given a number of potential premises, the rules of inference do not tell us which one to apply our rules first. For actual reasoning, we need over and above rules of inference also strategic rules, that is, rules that tell us how to apply the rules of inference. A realistic comparison between human thinking and information processing by computers should be conducted by reference to their ability to handle strategic rules, not by reference to the totality of theorems that can be proved mechanically.

70

Literature

Gödel's collected works are being edited by an editorial board headed by Solomon Feferman under the title *Collected Works* (Oxford University Press, New York). So far, three volumes have appeared: Vol. 1, *Publications 1929-1936, 1986*; Vol. 2, *Publications 1938-1974, 1990*; Vol. 3, *Unpublished Essays and Letters, 1995.* Gödel's German writings appear there in the original language and in English translation. These volumes include informative introductions and comments on the different writings by specialists. Other previously unpublished material has appeared in Kurt Gödel, *Unpublished Philosophical Essays,* ed. by Francisco A. Rodriguez-Consuegra (Birkhäuser, Basel, 1995). The original publications of Gödel's most important papers and monographs are as follows:

"Die Vollständigkeit des Axiome der logischen Funktionenkalküls," *Monatshefte für Mathematik und Physik* vol. 37 (1930), pp. 349-360.

"Über formal unentscheidbare Sätze der Principia Mathematica und verwandter Systeme I," *Monatshefte für Mathematik und Physik* vol. 38 (1931), pp. 173-198.

The Consistency of the Continuum Hypothesis (Princeton University Press, Princeton, New Jersey, 1940).

"What is Cantor's Continuum Problem?" *The American Mathematical Monthly* vol. 54 (1947), pp. 515-525.

"Über eine bisher noch nicht benützte Erweiterung des Finiten Standpunktes" *Dialectica*, vol. 12, (1958), pp. 280-287.

"Russell's Mathematical Logic," in *The Philosophy of Bertrand Russell* (Library of Living Philosophers), edited by Paul A. Schilpp (Northwestern University Press, Evanston, Ill., 1944) pp.123-153.

Gödel's personality, life and philosophical ideas have been extensively described and discussed by his friend Hao Wang in the two volumes *Reflections on Kurt Gödel* (MIT Press, Cambridge MA, 1987) and *A Logical Journey: From Gödel to Philosophy* (MIT Press, Cambridge, 1996). There is a good biography of Gödel, viz. John W. Dawson, Jr., *Logical Dilemmas: The Life and Work of Kurt Gödel* (A.K. Peters, Wellesley MA, 1997). Some biographical material on Kurt Gödel plus an article on his ideas about intuitionist logic were published as *Gödel Remembered (Salzburg 10-12 July 1983)*, edited by P. Weingartner and L. Schmetter (Bibliopolis, Napoli, 1987).

Good discussions of Gödel's work and its place in contemporary logic and foundations of mathematics are found in Solomon Feferman, "Gödel's Life and Work" and "Kurt Gödel: Conviction and Caution" in Solomon Feferman, *In the Light of Logic* (Oxford University Press, NewYork, 1998), pp. 127-149 and 150-164, as well as in Georg Kreisel, "Kurt Gödel 1906-1978", *Biographical Memoirs of Fellows of the Royal Society* vol. 26 (December 1980), pp. 148 – 224.

Reliable but technical explicit expositions of Gödel's incompleteness results are found among other places in Andrzej Mostowski, *Sentences Undecidable in Formalized Arithmetic: An Exposition of the Theory of Kurt Gödel* (North-Holland, Amsterdam, 1952) and more recently in C. Smorynski, "The Incompleteness Theorems" in Jon Barwise, editor, *Handbook of Mathematical Logic* (North-Holland, Amsterdam, 1977), pp. 821-866, and last but not least Raymond M. Smullyan, *Gödel's Incompleteness Theorems* (Oxford University Press, New York, 1992). Smullyan has also given popular (and funny) but at the same time accurate expositions of Gödel-type reasoning in his puzzle books, especially in *What Is the Name of This Book* (Prentice-Hall, Englewood Cliffs, New Jersey, 1978).

Solomon Feferman's work on Gödel's second incompleteness theorem is presented in a sequence of important papers, beginning with "Arithmetization of Metamathematics in General Setting," *Fundamenta Mathematicae* vol. 49 (1960), pp. 35-92. A useful brief survey of this work is given in Feferman's paper "My Route to Arithmetization," *Theoria* vol. 63 (1997), pp. 168-181.

Alfred Tarski's early writings parallel to some extent Gödel's. They are accessible in the collection *Logic, Semantics, Metamathematics* (Clarendon Press, Oxford, 1956).

Chaitin's speculations are presented among other places in G.J. Chaitin, "Information-Theoretic Limitations of Formal Systems", *Journal of the Association for Computing Machinery* vol. 21 (1982), pp. 941-954. The hollowness of Chaitin's claims is shown in Panu Raatikainen, "On Interpreting Chaitin's Incompleteness Theorems", *Journal of Philosophical Logic* vol. 27 (1998), pp. 569-586.

There are excellent source books covering the developments in logic and in the foundations of mathematics that form the background of Gödel's work, including Jean von Heinjenoort, *From Frege to Gödel* (Harvard U.P., 1967) and William B. Ewald, *From Kant to Hilbert, I-II* (Oxford U.P., 1996).

For the difference between first-order and higher-order logic and the different interpretations of the latter see Jaakko Hintikka, "Standard vs. Nonstandard Distinction: A Watershed in the Foundations of Mathematics", in Jaakko Hintikka, editor, *From Dedekind to Gödel* (Kluwer Academic, Dordrecht, 1995), pp. 21-44.

The exposition of the results mentioned at the end of Chapter 5 is found in J. Paris and L. Harrington, "A Mathematical Incompleteness in Peano Arithmetic" in Jon Barwise, editor, *Handbook of Mathematical Logic* (North-Holland, Amsterdam, 1977), pp.1133-1142.

Gentzen's papers are collected in M.E. Szabo, editor, *The Collected Papers of Gerhard Gentzen* (North-Holland, Amsterdam, 1969).

Paul Cohen's work in set theory (as well as most of Gödel's work) summarized in Paul Cohen, *Set Theory and the Continuum Hypothesis* (W. A. Benjamin, New York and Amsterdam, 1966). For the axiom of choice, see Gregory H. Moore, *Zermelo's Axioms of Choice* (Springer, Heidelberg and New York, 1982). For the continuum hypothesis see Raymond Smullyan and Melvin Fitting, *Set Theory and the Continuum Problem* (Oxford University Press, 1996).

The basic papers by Gödel, Church, Turing, Rosser, Kleene and Post have been reprinted in Martin Davis, editor, *The Undecidable* (Raven Press, Hewlett, New York, 1965).

The discussion about the possible significance of Gödel's incompleteness theorem for the question whether a human mind can be a machine was started by John R. Lucas, "Minds, Machines and Gödel", *Philosophy* vol. 36 (1961), pp. 112-127. (See also J.R. Lucas, "Mind, Machines and Gödel; a Retrospect", in P.J.R. Millican and A. Clark, *Machines and Thought* (Clarendon Press, Oxford, 1996) pp.103-124. Lucas was responding to Alan Turing's classical article "Computing Machinery and Intelligence", *Mind* vol. 59 (1950), pp. 433-460. The subsequent literature on this problem is as extensive as it is inconclusive. The battle has even been joined by prominent mathematicians and scientists like Roger Penrose in his books *The Emperor's New Mind* (Oxford University Press, New York, 1989) and *Shadows of the Mind* (Oxford University Press, New York, 1994). As far as Gödel's own ideas of the subject are concerned, the best guide is Hao Wang, "Can Machines Think?", *Philosophia Mathematica,* series 3, vol. 1 (1993), pp. 97-138. An informed and judicious discussion of the whole range of related issues is found in Judson Webb, "Metamathematics and the Philosophy of Mind", *Science* vol. 35 (1968), pp. 156-178, and in his *Mechanism, Mentalism and Metamathematics* (D. Reidel, Dordrecht, 1980